ORDER IN THE COURT

How You Can Enjoy an Orderly Life

ORDER IN THE COURT

How You Can Enjoy an Orderly Life

Sherry Hutson Camperson

SWORD of the LORD
PUBLISHERS
P.O. BOX 1099, MURFREESBORO, TN 37133

Printed and Bound in the United States of America

FOREWORD

Dr. Bob Jones, Sr., used to say, "Life is not divided into the secular and sacred. All ground is holy ground, and every bush is a burning bush."

Of course, Dr. Jones was right. The Scripture says in Colossians 3:17,23: "And whatsoever ye do in word or deed, do all in the name of the Lord Jesus, giving thanks to God and the Father by him"; "And whatsoever ye do, do it heartily, as to the Lord, and not unto men." Whether singing in the choir, giving the baby a bath or cleaning the house, we're to do it all as unto the Lord.

If two people have the exact same abilities and one is a Christian while the other is not, then the one who is a Christian ought to do a better job simply because of the fact that she or he is a Christian. When it comes to order in the home, then the Christian home ought to be better organized and more orderly than the non-Christian home.

Here is a book filled with holy, helpful hints on how to be better organized in almost every area of your life, beginning with some good, spiritual advice up front. After all, if the heart is not right, it is not likely that the head and hands will follow.

The unorganized person will experience frustration, a drain on energies, a waste of time and usually general dissatisfaction. My father used to say, "A place for everything and everything in its place."

This lecture was first given by our oldest daughter Sherry Camperson to a group of ladies at one of our Sword Women's Jubilees. When she had finished, nearly every lady present asked if she had copies of the material she shared; and Sherry explained that she really had not shared all the material that she had prepared. Immediately the ladies began to ask her to put it into print, so this book is the fulfillment of that request.

v

You'll discover a wealth of information in this book, and you'll be surprised at the thorough preparations made by its author.

By the way, I'm happy to see that Sherry has dedicated the book to her mother. Mrs. Hutson and I have been married now for more than forty-one years, and I say without reservation that she must be one of the most organized people in the world. By keeping our home clean and beautiful, she has added much to my ministry. I've never been embarrassed to take people into our home nor to invite them for a meal because I knew that the home would be in order. Of course, Mrs. Hutson would probably disagree, saying that this is not right or that is not right; but that's because she always wants everything to be "just right."

Here's a good book to give to the new bride or to teach to young single ladies who are looking forward to marriage. It is also a book for any housewife who would like better to organize her home, her heart and her life.

Buy a copy for yourself and give a copy to a friend. It is "bound to be" a blessing (pun intended).

—Curtis Hutson
Editor, SWORD OF THE LORD

ACKNOWLEDGMENT

I am the grateful product of the sacrifices, multiplied by the time and energy, charitably donated by the blessed people God has sent to coordinate the points of my life. I'm the stark contrast of a self-made woman, if in fact there is such a thing.

Some have fashioned the fabric of my life through many years of patiently weaving just one thread at a time. Others have added contrast and hue as their bright and colorful lives "bled" on mine. You know who you are, and you know how grateful I am.

While thankful for the many who made their slight *impressions* from a distance, my deepest gratitude goes to those select few who took the risk and the time to make their solid *impact* really close up.

Helen Steiner Rice beautifully expresses my sincere sentiment in this all-encompassing acknowledgment:

> People everywhere in life
> From every walk and station,
> From every town and city
> And every state and nation
> Have given me so many things
> Intangible and dear,
> I couldn't begin to count them all
> Or even make them clear....
> I only know I owe so much
> To people everywhere
> And when I put my thoughts in words
> It's just a way to share
> The musings of a thankful heart,
> A heart much like your own,
> For nothing that I think or write
> Is mine and mine alone....
> So if you found some blessing
> In any word or line,
> It's just your soul's reflection
> In proximity with mine.
> —Used by permission

INTRODUCTION

One cannot live in a haphazard manner and pray that everything will come out right in the end. The ideas and suggestions shared here are offered to you for your selective use. You will probably never use all of them, and you'll certainly not use them all at once.

Each job you tackle as a woman will require its own "set of tools." But instead of cramming your hands full by grabbing for all these tools at once, which will essentially halt your work, just pick up that one "tool" that best fits your hand. Try it, and see how it works.

But tools are only tools. They must be plugged into the right power source. Draw on the power of Christ within you and make those "home improvements" a little at a time. God will encourage and reward your every effort in search of order and peace. He will welcome your company, for His abode is order and peace. And you will find greater enjoyment in living.

And be reminded that "duties never conflict" (Bob Jones, Sr.). There is no level of organization high enough and no management of time strict enough to grant any individual a proficient performance of tasks that God did not assign.

I was comforted and encouraged when I realized that Proverbs 31 is not a listing of the Ideal Woman's daily activities. No—she didn't get up before the sun, purchase a nice piece of property, plant a vineyard, make bread, shop for wool and flax, then weave cloth, stitch the children's clothes, run errands for her husband, take food to the hungry, market her fine linen, look like a million dollars, speak sagely and stay up all night—each and every day of her life.

Proverbs 31:10-31 is a summary of her entire life! I don't feel guilty anymore, and neither should you. There were seasons to her life, just as there are seasons to our lives.

Dr. and Mrs. Curtis Hutson

DEDICATION

In Honor of Mrs. Curtis Hutson, My Mother

A Tribute to Her Example and Expertise
as a Homemaker

Keeper at Home

Her work is done behind the scenes—
    No fanfare or great show.
She does the duties left unseen
    As though the world would know.

No task's too small to leave undone
    Or do with little vim.
Her home's a palace fair to all,
    But 'specially to HIM!

The good works that she does reach out
    Beyond her own abode;
She showers deeds of kindliness
    To all upon life's road.

Her motherhood is also known;
    Her children rise up here
And say that of all womenfolk
    She's blessed and most dear.

—Becky Vradenburgh

Order in the Court

How You Can Enjoy an Orderly Life

Sherry's workshop was presented April 11, 1992 during the Sword of the Lord Women's Jubilee at Franklin Road Baptist Church in Murfreesboro, Tennessee. Because the theme was "Daughters of the King," she entitled her workshop, "Order in the Court."

In Honor of Mrs. Curtis Hutson, My Mother
A Tribute to Her Example and Expertise
as a Homemaker

Mother was present during the delivery of this workshop. Speaking on the subject of housekeeping with her in the audience was as intimidating as speaking on the topic of shipbuilding with Noah in the audience.

On a scale of 1 to 10, 10 being the best, Mother rates a 20. She, being the expert, should have been standing and giving instruction. But she says she doesn't speak. Now Daddy may disagree with *that* statement! But, seriously, she chooses not to speak publicly, so I spoke *for* her.

She will read this book with great interest and enthusiasm. Her continuing desire to learn and improve is one of her secrets to success as a homemaker. New and fresh ideas add even more excitement to her already fulfilling role as wife of Dr. Curtis Hutson.

We are forever sharing books and articles on this subject, keeping one another challenged as homemakers. Mother is "always teaching and always teachable." I learned most everything I know about homemaking while growing up in the orderly environment she provided for me. So as a tribute to her example and expertise, I lovingly present: *Order in the Court.*

Much prayer has prefaced this presentation. I've asked the Lord to help me be an encouragement and not just an informant. The last time-management workshop I attended was about six hours in duration, and I was overwhelmed as I sheepishly walked out. I felt as if I'd failed to get even a sip of water from a fire hydrant.

My desire is to blend inspiration with practical helps in such a way that you will realize you *can* have an orderly life and enjoy the many benefits of such a victorious lifestyle. When you complete this material, may you feel hopeful that an orderly life is achievable and worth the up-front sacrifices that are required to make it possible. May this short reading be an investment of your time—not a waste of it.

The gamut of home management will certainly not be exhausted in these few pages; and even some of the very basics will not be addressed. Included in this succinct summary are only those general guidelines and specific suggestions that have worked wonderfully for others and me. I've added a list of books on this topic for further reading at the end of this text.

As all women, I perform several different roles. I am the wife of Rick Camperson, pastor of Gwinnett County Baptist Church. I am mother to Alan, Curt and Jana Kay. I am the firstborn (notice I chose not to say "oldest") child of Dr. and Mrs. Curtis Hutson. And I treasure the titles of aunt, sister, pastor's wife, teacher, friend and servant, too.

ORDER IN THE COURT

And, oh, how I do love the role of homemaker! Even when filling out forms, I enjoy writing, "Occupation: homemaker." I hope the joy I experience as a homemaker will tie these pages all together and renew your love for this very noble profession—for that it truly is!

❂ ❂ ❂ ❂ ❂

God is a God of order. He, being the ultimate example of orderliness, has a plan and purpose for everything He created; and everything is always in its proper place. Psalm 19:1, 2 speaks of His "handywork." *Handywork* literally means "fingerwork or handcraft" in the Hebrew language of the Old Testament. His marvelous Creation is to Him nothing more than "needlework" we might carry around in a totebag to work on in our spare time.

Each creative work of God has purpose, but it also has beauty. The flower is an intricate system with great purpose in our ecosystem, but it is beautiful as well. And, oh, how the changing leaves of fall add beauty to the landscape of autumn!

We drove through a terrible rainstorm on the way to our grandfather's funeral in South Carolina. Daddy and I were talking about the storm. He made a statement that I pondered for several miles: "You know, there is the same amount of water today as there was when God created the earth."

I thought, *Of course. Before the Flood, it didn't rain, but the earth was covered in a vapor canopy. And today without the vapor canopy, that same water evaporates and condensates in the form of clouds. Then rain falls, and that same water sinks back into the ground.*

And so the cycle continues. Scientists call this the Law of the Conservation of Matter. You might say God is into recycling.

Then Daddy said, "There is no such thing as a universal drought. While it might be very dry in California, it might be flooding in Texas." I could see the "wheels turning" in

3

Mother's mind. In her humorous way she said, "If it is raining this hard here, it must be really dry somewhere else."

In the Gospels, Jesus used His organizational skills to help others. There are many examples, but the feeding of the five thousand is one that stands out to me. You think feeding your family is a big task—and it is. But imagine—five thousand hungry mouths—more, since women and children were not included in that count. Jesus broke up this big job into manageable bits by grouping the people by fifties and hundreds. And, you know, He was not wasteful. He had the disciples collect all the leftovers; and He didn't even need them!

I prefer using the word *order* over *organization*. *Order* is a Bible word. I don't recall the words *organize* or *organization* being in the Scriptures. But *order* is found many times, especially describing the details of the Tabernacle.

Organize tends to be a divisive word. By that I mean, people assume they are either born with the ability to organize or they were not so blessed. It is true that some are born with certain God-given talents. And some even receive the "grace gift" or "spiritual gift" of organization at their spiritual birth.

One lady told me how her little five-year-old boy, upon entering a department store, would proceed to the clothes racks and begin sorting the sweaters and shirts by colors. Our own little Jana Kay practices similar arrangements. You may have noticed such traits in the children you love. So, yes, it is true that "organization" plays favorites and is a "respecter of persons."

Because this is true, I opt for the word *order*. Orderliness is commanded in the Scriptures and does not exclude any one of us. Order calls for character adjustment rather than talent, giftedness, ability or skill.

While it is fairly feasible to *establish* order, the chilling challenge is in *keeping* order. That is why we call it: housekeeping. Joan Rivers, not my favorite personality, said the reason she hates housekeeping is that, once you get everything cleaned, you have to do it all over again six months later. Well, I should hope she cleans her house or has it cleaned more often than that. But she expressed the frustration of many homemakers.

"Keeping house" is a little like spinning plates on sticks. You get one plate spinning—the laundry. Get the next plate spinning—supper; next plate—children; next plate—pay the bills. Now your husband needs attention. There seem to be too many plates. By the time all the plates are finally spinning, you look back and—oops! That first plate is wobbling. Run back and give it another spin. We all have plates to spin —yes, all different, but there is a common pattern.

Maintaining order in the midst of a hustle, bustle world is a little like spinning plates in a circus. However, this is serious business—not monkey business. We are called upon to fill a professional role. The titles, Home Executive and Household Engineer, may be more fitting than Homemaker.

God starts on the inside and works out. We'll follow His pattern. Order on the outside must be a reflection and overflow of order on the inside.

ORDER IN THE HEART

James 4:1 asks, "From whence come wars and fightings among you? come they not hence, even of your lusts that war in your members?" Confusion on the outside means there's confusion on the inside. Order and peace on the outside will be the natural result of order and peace on the inside.

Some of my favorite authors on order and housekeeping have recently written books about what they call "the inside job." The hilarious sister team, Pam Young and Peggy Jones, authors of *The Sidetracked Home Executive*, have a newer book called *The Happiness File*. They know the importance of organization—that organization is not an end in itself but the means to a happy life of service for God and others.

Anne Ortlund, whose writings I enjoy, recently shared her heart in *Disciplines of the Heart*. Renowned for her organizational skills spelled out in *Disciplines of the Beautiful Woman*, she revealed the deeper purposes for order in her newer publication.

"*Keep thy heart* with all diligence; for out of it are the issues of life" (Proverbs 4:23). Of the myriad Christ-honoring attitudes the heart can house, certain heart conditions are especially conducive to an orderly life. Let's strive for them. "The king's daughter is all glorious within. . ." (Psalm 45:13).

Cleansed Heart

"Create in me a clean heart, O God; and renew a right spirit within me" (Psalm 51:10). A cleansed heart comes only through the cleansing blood of Jesus Christ. Perhaps your heart has not been cleansed—you have never experienced salvation. Your life is a total disaster then; you need to start at square one. Receiving Christ as your Saviour is the most important step you will ever take—the most important decision you will ever make.

First John 1:7 says, ". . .the blood of Jesus Christ his Son cleanseth us from all sin."

> Were all the seas water
> And all the land soap;
> If Thy blood not wash me,
> There is no hope!

Jesus is your only hope of salvation. Will you receive Him today?

After salvation, our heart requires a daily cleansing through confession of sin in prayer. "If we confess our sins, he is faithful and just to forgive us our sins, and to cleanse us from all unrighteousness" (I John 1:9).

Bible reading cleanses the heart, too. "Now ye are clean through the word which I have spoken unto you" (John 15:3).

Daddy gave an illustration years ago about a woman questioning the benefit of reading the Scriptures. She said, "I'd just as well not read the Bible because I can't remember what I read anyhow. And I don't understand a lot of what I can remember." A wise friend told her, "Well, your mind is like a sieve or a sifter. You may not be able to retain it all, but the water (God's Word is compared to water) running through the sifter will keep it clean."

A young mother was struggling. She had three babies, just one year separating them. Sapped of her energy and further weakened by missing her Bible-reading and prayer time, she was despondent. "I must have my time with the Lord," she cried. But each day from the moment the children awakened, she could not find the time she so desperately needed. Determined, she set her alarm clock for 2:00 in the morning. So from 2:00 a.m. to 3:00 a.m. she claimed her quiet time with the Lord. This was Mommy's 2:00 o'clock feeding! We must strive this diligently for a clean heart.

Contented Heart

"No matter how palatial the home in which we live, we still dwell in tents—con*tent* or discon*tent*" (SWORD OF THE LORD).

"Let your conversation be without covetousness; and be content with such things as ye have. . ." (Hebrews 13:5).

Advertising is designed to make us discontent with what we have. Satan often uses this tactic to scuttle our system of organization. What do I mean? Well, you must be content with what you have—your home, car, belongings, etc.—before you will be motivated to spend your valuable time keeping them orderly.

If I'm not happy and content with what I have now, I'll not

be happy and content when I get what I think I want. Ecclesiastes 5:10 says, "He that loveth silver shall not be satisfied with silver."

Realize that you already have everything you need for your present happiness. If I am always projecting myself into the future with statements like "I can be a good housekeeper when I get a bigger house" or "I can be more organized when I have more storage space," then I have sunk my own ship. "It is not what she has which expresses the worth of a woman, but what she is" (Henri Frederic Amiel).

Contentment will ward off feelings of jealousy and envy and will free us from trying to "keep up with the Joneses." Envy is feeling bad when someone else prospers, desiring to deprive that one of what she has. On the other hand, the jealous one wants the desirable object for herself. Some types of jealousy are godly. This type of jealousy is the child of love, but envy is always the child of hate.

Paul said in Philippians 4:11, ". . .I have learned, in whatsoever state I am, therewith to be content."

Are you content with what you have and where you are at this time in your life? Be encouraged by what Paul said. Contentment is a *learned* character quality. If you are discontent, take heart. You can learn to be content; you are not trapped. If you can't have the best of everything, then make the best of everything you have.

Cheerful Heart

"A merry heart maketh a cheerful countenance: but by sorrow of the heart the spirit is broken" (Proverbs 15:13). You can work better with a cheerful attitude, now, can't you?

Moses' work was hindered and other serious consequences followed when he lost the joy of his work. Remember the circumstances in which Moses became tired and worn out? He no longer enjoyed his work as the leader of the Israelites.

Moses began to delegate his own God-given responsibilities

to people God had not chosen to bear them. First Moses shared his responsibility of speaking with Aaron, and this compromise ended up with the people molding and worshiping the golden calf.

Then Moses shared his responsibility of judging with many newly appointed assistants, after which many of his people were destroyed by fire. Next Moses delegated the responsibility of counseling to seventy assignees, whose inception was the beginning of the Sanhedrin. This official body shared in Christ's crucifixion years later. Serious consequences follow a loss of joy in one's work.

Paul reinforces this point: "That ye might walk worthy of the Lord unto all pleasing. . . . Strengthened with all might, according to his glorious power, unto all patience and long-suffering with *joyfulness*" (Colossians 1:10,11).

As a woman, you set the atmosphere of your home, workplace or other surroundings. We all have our "ups-and-downs." But a mother can't afford herself the luxury of wallowing in depression. Our children are looking to see if God's grace really is sufficient for our needs.

I was in the laundry room facing that mundane morning chore, unaware of my moans and groans aggravating the atmosphere. Later in the afternoon I met up again with the now clean clothes and was singing as I folded the dry ones.

A young but strong arm rested on my shoulder. It was Alan, our older son. "Now, that's better, Mother." He who had felt the weight of my "heavy heart" was relieved to hear me now happily praising the Lord with a song. You know, I hadn't even noticed that he was paying attention. When you are sad, your family and friends are, too.

Sir James Barrie said, "The secret of happiness is not in doing what one likes to do, but in liking what one has to do."

Contrite Heart

"A broken and a contrite heart, O God, thou wilt not

9

despise" (Psalm 51:17). In this verse *contrite* means "collapsed or crouched." I qualify, do you?

Wouldn't you agree that we must have the presence and power of God in order to fulfill the responsibilities of managing a household? We must have His very Person within so that we can develop the quality of orderliness.

Where does He dwell? "For thus saith the high and lofty One. . .whose name is Holy; I dwell. . .with him also that is of a contrite and humble spirit" (Isaiah 57:15a). In the first part of this verse, *contrite* means "crushed."

The latter part of the verse tells us how we can be rejuvenated, revived, given a new vision. I dwell within "to revive the spirit of the humble, and to revive the heart of the contrite ones" (Isaiah 57:15b). Here *contrite* means "crumbled or bruised, beaten to pieces." Sometimes I feel this way, too.

"The Lord is nigh unto them that are of a broken heart; and saveth such as be of a contrite spirit" (Psalm 34:18).

Let's not lose out by refusing our Help and pushing Him away with a proud, self-sufficient attitude. "God resisteth the proud, but giveth grace unto the humble" (James 4:6).

Controlled Heart

"And be not drunk with wine, wherein is excess; but be filled with the Spirit" (Ephesians 5:18). This proclamation wields a powerful prodding for me in particular.

My parents gave me the name Sherry at birth. At that time they'd never heard that parents should attach aspiring and meaningful names to their children. When Daddy was made aware of this, he looked up the meaning of my name in hopes that it would be a suitable title for his little girl.

What a shock it was for him to learn that Sherry means "intoxicated or drunk"! Why, what had they done? "Surely our daughter won't live up to her name!" Being the wise man that he is, he presented me with a godly challenge: "Sweetheart, your name literally means 'drunk.' But let's attach this Bible verse to it: 'Be not drunk with wine, wherein is excess; but be filled with the Spirit.' " Now, I liked that.

At one point in my life, I might have erroneously and futilely mustered up *self*-control that I might fulfill my responsibilities. Self-control is good and profitable (Proverbs 16:32). But I know that my battles are far greater than my self-control alone can conquer. I must be controlled by the Holy Spirit.

> Thousands of women fall into the strong-hearted, stoic class. You may quite unknowingly be depriving yourself of God's best for you by making use of your own willpower and calling it Christianity. You may be right in your thinking, but if you are in control of your own personality, the stronger your will, the redder will become your face as you hammer mercilessly. But if you have acted under His control, then the total responsibility rests with Him! —Eugenia Price, used by permission.

A cleansed heart. A contented heart. A cheerful heart. A contrite heart. And a controlled heart. We must develop and nourish these conditions of the heart so that we might display order in our outward appearance and surroundings.

While it is certain that "the Lord seeth not as man seeth. . . but. . .looketh on the heart," it is also for sure and for certain that "man looketh on the outward appearance" (I Samuel 16:7).

See the Great Judge as He brings down His gavel: "Let all things be done decently and in order" (I Corinthians 14:40). We are talking clear command here, not simply suggestion.

ORDER IN THE COURT

So how would you describe your home? Is there order in the court, or is the palace a royal mess?

"The aged women likewise. . .That they may teach the young

ORDER IN THE COURT

women to be sober [proper self-estimation], *to love their husbands, to love their children, To be discreet, chaste,* **keepers at home**, *good, obedient to their own husbands, that the word of God be not blasphemed."*—Titus 2:3-5.

You don't pay the price for order; you enjoy the benefits of an orderly life. Hopefully the following list of benefits that come along with order will motivate you to finish perusing these pages.

Just how will you benefit?

1. You'll reap God's blessings. Orderliness is a character quality God tells you to develop. Obedience will prove to bring His blessings. God wants to bless your life with true happiness. "If ye know these things, happy are ye if ye do them" (John 13:17).

2. You'll share life with a happy husband. Most men want their homes in "apple-pie" order with a fresh apple pie cooling on the kitchen table.

3. You'll feel relief from needless pressure and stress. The Philadelphia *Daily News* published an article from the Headache Center of the Germantown Hospital entitled, "Old-Fashioned Tips Can Relieve Stress." One suggestion was: "Create order out of chaos. Organize your home and work area so you always know where things are. You'll avoid the stress of losing things."

4. You'll discover time for activities you enjoy the most. Doing housework the hard way is for people who have nothing better to do. Some are averse to this notion of orderliness, mistakenly thinking their time will be consumed with organizing. The very opposite is true. You'll find more time for your walk with God and for knowing Him better. And more time will be available for others you love—your family and friends.

5. You'll share hospitality more spontaneously and more often. Hospitality is a qualification for a bishop or pastor and an ornament to any Christian home. Romans

ORDER IN THE COURT

12:10, 13 talks of being "given to hospitality." Before studying this expression, "given to," I thought hospitality was somewhat of a passive attitude. My home was available if a missionary came through town or a college student needed a room for the weekend. But I had the wrong idea. Hospitality is active, not passive. "Given to" means "to run someone down." When was the last time you ran somebody down to show hospitality?

6. You'll save money when you can eliminate "emergency buying" and concentrate on "intentional spending." You will be able to find your coupons, rebates, etc., and use them before the expiration dates.

7. You'll free your mind of clutter. Even if you don't acutely feel the drain of confusion, it is nonetheless depleting your emotional energy. Your mind is subconsciously keeping up with each and every unnecessary item.

8. You'll escape needless depression. Poor housekeeping will lead to despondency and the feeling of being out of control.

9. You'll uncover creativity that you didn't know you had. An orderly environment stimulates creativity and thinking.

10. You'll raise orderly children. Young children need a schedule for security and training. Only through their parents' orderly lives can evolve happy, obedient, orderly children. I am very thankful that I was nurtured in a home where both mother and father were orderly and organized. What a wonderful habitat I call home!

"Let all things be done decently and in order" (I Corinthians 14:40). *Decently* means in a graceful manner.

In charm school young girls are taught to be graceful—that is, to perform each task with the least amount of motion. A graceful performance is a task done efficiently. This, of course, is the opposite of clamorous, boisterous and clumsy.

ORDER IN THE COURT

The word *order* in this verse simply means "arrangement." This is the opposite of confusion.

I've been told that for every Bible principle there exists a balancing truth in God's Word. On this subject of order, we can clearly see the principle *and* the balancing truth. God demands orderliness, but He balances this demand with His plea for moderation.

"Let your moderation be known unto all men. The Lord is at hand" (Philippians 4:5). The picture word for *moderation* is a reminder I need. *Moderation* means "sweet reasonableness and balance." (I am struck with conviction just now. Seldom am I sweet when I am forced to sweep the floor yet again. And I'm not always reasonable with expectations for our very young children.)

We must be reasonable and establish boundaries even in this area of orderliness. The character flaw of perfectionism is a hindrance in my own life, as I try to obey Philippians 4:5.

Balance is so important. Anything unbalanced is about to fall. Organization—out of balance—can become an idol. Anything that takes all your mind and energy is an idol. Yes, organization can become a false god.

Now that I've included this "disclaimer," let's continue our quiet quest for the quintessence of our subject.

We'll need a plan. Charles Spurgeon said, "Dig a well before you are thirsty." Proverbs 2:11 says, "Discretion shall preserve thee. . . ." In the Hebrew dictionary, *discretion* means "a plan." A paraphrase of this verse might read, "A plan shall protect you from getting distracted or failing." I like to think that planning helps me to invest my time rather than just to spend it.

A wise general always draws up his battle plan before he meets up with the enemy. Be alerted that Satan, our enemy, ever lurks to scrap our best efforts. The wise general doesn't postpone basic decisions until the bullets are fired. He is also prepared to change his plans if an emergency calls for it.

14

ORDER IN THE COURT

D. L. Moody said, "Always be prepared." Moody illustrates with the story of a German general. When war was declared between France and Germany, Count von Moltke, this German general, was prepared for it. Word was brought to him late at night after he had gone to bed. "Take the third portfolio on the left," said the general. "Very well," replied the messenger. Count von Moltke easily went back to sleep. He had done his planning ahead of time (*The Life of D. L. Moody*, p. 491, Sword of the Lord Publishers).

Planning is a mindset—continually looking ahead and preparing for the future no matter how close or how distant that future may be. What can I do today about tomorrow, next week or next month? We tend to over-plan the present and under-plan the long range.

That is why big events, like Christmas, are difficult for most of us. Instead of doing a little bit at a time throughout the year, we try to cram too much into a short period of time. This ends up hurting the whole family.

Mr. Greenwalt, former president of Dupont Company, said that one minute spent in planning saves three or four minutes in execution. He added, "If an executive is too busy to stop and plan, he may find himself replaced by another man who takes the time to plan."

In Mark 1:35 we find a clue to the success of Jesus' work. What did He do in His busy morning? ". . .a great while before day, he went out, and departed into a solitary place, and there prayed." He prayerfully planned His day, waiting on His knees for His Father's instructions.

Jesus lived life day by day just like we do. He didn't have a detailed drawn-out blueprint to follow. He discerned His Father's will day by day in a life of prayer. But He had a plan.

We, too, need a plan. But we must let God alter it as He sees fit. "Father knows best."

My prayer is that of a well-known preacher, "Help me not to be hurried or rushed, for my schedule is in Your Hands. Help me not to leave a trail of tension and apprehension. Help me

to leave tracks of peace and stability everywhere I go."
We don't want our tombstone to read: "Worried, hurried and buried."
You will need a plan; but you, along with your family, are custom-built. Your lifestyle is a unique combination of scores of variables: your marital status, the number and ages of your children, the type and size of your housing, and you and/or your husband's job schedule. You may be a stay-at-home mom or one who has to work outside the home.

You may be the caretaker of extended family members with health needs, or you may have a spouse or child with specific nutritional requirements. Our younger son Curt has a wheat allergy, which changes my cooking style for him. Our niece, Denielle, has diabetes; so my sister, Donna, prepares special meals designed just for her. And our daddy is fighting cancer holistically, so Mother's meal-planning is based on his individual nutritional needs.

No one-size-fits-all plan will work for every family. Come to think of it, I've never seen a one-size-fits-all garment that wore nicely on anyone either. Is there really such a thing?

Each family is different, meeting different deadlines, shuffling different schedules, reaching for different goals and sporting different interests that all change as the family grows. There is no right or wrong way.

The following pages are not filled with "shoulds" but "suggestions." The information is practical and to the point. What follows is a compendium of ideas that have helped lift my load as a woman trying to serve God and the precious people that He has so graciously put into my life. This section may serve as a reference of sorts or a resource that you can reread from time to time.

CALENDAR/NOTEBOOK

"So teach us to number our days, that we may apply our hearts unto wisdom" (Psalm 90:12). There is a need to

ORDER IN THE COURT

visualize time—"to number our days." A clock and a calendar are the only ways I know to do that. Hang a clock somewhere in each room of your house so you will be aware of the fleeting moments. Post a large calendar in that area of your home where each family member will see it and check it often.

THE NOTEBOOK—For the last sixteen years, I have carried an organizer/notebook. It is about the size of my Bible and easy to carry. Through the years, I have worn out several. My favorite is a Franklin Quest leather binding with handles for carrying. An enclosing zipper protects loose items from falling out. It holds standard 8 1/2 by 5 1/2 filler paper. A "completely furnished" notebook can cost as little as $10.00 or as much as $100.00, depending on the quality of the binding and details of the body. While browsing through a luxurious luggage store, I found some that were even more than $100.00.

I am seldom seen without mine. My husband calls it my "brain." So when I drop it and papers are strewn across the floor, I'm "scatter-brained."

We visited a family one evening, and I left my notebook there. Rick said, "Oh, my! Now you've lost your 'mind'!" It was a forty-five-minute drive, but we made a beeline back to find it. Why, no one can live without his "brain"!

This notebook becomes the memory that you cannot retain. Write it all down. A dull pencil is better than a sharp mind. You won't waste emotional and mental energy trying to remember if you just write it down "on site." And you will need to know where you put what you write down. Ahha!—the notebook. You now have your own private secretary.

NOTEBOOK SECTIONS—Your notebook will be tailor-made. It will be composed of sections to meet your individual needs. Just for an example, my notebook is divided into the following sections:

Calendar: When I first set up this system, I designed my own calendar pages. But today I choose from the several systems available at office supply stores. I order the Day-

17

Timers model with the month-at-a-glance pages, along with daily sheets printed in a timeline format.

I keep three months ahead with the month-at-a-glance pages and insert daily sheets behind the current month only. When making an appointment for the near future, I write the time, place, phone number, directions, what to bring, etc., on that daily sheet.

If the event is in the distant future, I pencil it in on the month-at-a-glance calendar. This way it can be erased if plans change, as they often do when made that far in advance. Then I transfer the information to my daily sheet when the time draws nearer.

Make an appointment with yourself each morning to look over the scheduled events, activities, phone calls and deadlines assigned to and planned for that day. I also like to look over tomorrow's plans the evening before.

This time is also my appointment with God. I keep my notebook with me when I'm having this quiet time of Bible reading and prayer. The notebook is used for jotting down thoughts and verses I want to remember.

The notebook serves another purpose during my daily appointment with God. The Devil likes to interrupt my thoughts by reminding me of what I have to do that day. He haunts me with the fear of forgetting something important. He knows he can distract my Bible and prayer time because my mind will be occupied until I write it down. So I keep that notebook nearby; and when Satan reminds me of an appointment or a promise I made, I say, "Thank you very much," pausing just long enough to write it down, and then continue reading with a clear mind.

How do we get where we're going on time? I'm feeling convicted, but we do need to ponder punctuality. Let's discuss "backward planning," a phrase Anne Ortlund coined. On your daily calendar make a notation of the time you will need to get ready to leave. Focus on this estimated time of departure (ETD), not the estimated time of arrival (ETA).

ORDER IN THE COURT

You will arrive at this time simply by planning in reverse. Your dental appointment is at 11:00 a.m. The trip takes 30 minutes. Fifteen minutes must be allotted for packing the car and buckling in the children. (You can see I have small children.) It will take you one hour to get bathed and dressed and another half hour to dress the children. So you must begin your preparations at 8:45 a.m.—no later, or you will be late. Focus on this hour rather than the time of your appointment. "Backward planning" will help you get there on time.

Keep a small basket near the exit door of your house to drop in those items you need to take along with you. My basket often has things in it like books to loan out or canned goods for a food drive. Sometimes it has tapes or CDs to loan out or return. Very often I drop in music I will need for special music practices at church or for the boys' music lessons. The basket is near the door; and when someone calls or I am prompted, I put the item in the basket immediately.

Goals and Projects: Here's where I keep record of progress on "running projects." These are projects that take more than one day. It would be a waste of time to rewrite them each day on the daily calendar pages.

"Running projects" include preparation for Christmas or redecorating a room. Goals include scripture passages or poems I'm trying to memorize. Keeping them in my notebook allows me to memorize while I am waiting for our boys during their music lessons.

Lists: This is one of the most helpful sections in my opinion. I am a list-maker. Do you know who the list-maker is in the Bible? I can identify with Agur, son of Jakeh. God used Agur to write Proverbs 30. In this rather short chapter, Agur made six lists. Read this chapter to find out the kinds of lists he made. By the way, his name means "gatherer." Now isn't that appropriate?

I used to have lists all over the house. But when it came time to go shopping, I couldn't find my grocery list or gift list.

ORDER IN THE COURT

I file my many lists in this section.

My lists include "To buy," "To do sometime," "To write" and "To thank." On this page I make note of whom I need to thank and why. It is not always necessary to send a prompt thank-you note. Sometimes it is more effective to express your sentiment a couple of weeks later. Your benefactor will know you are still enjoying and appreciating his kindness to you.

"List of menus." When Curt was born, Mother stayed with us for a week. She wrote out nineteen delicious menus in her own handwriting. I use this original list to help compile yet another list—a "Grocery list." Type up a basic grocery list with the layout of your market in mind. We buy about the same things each week, don't we? This typed list will save you time since you won't have to handwrite the same list over each week. It will also serve as a reminder to pick up items that you may have forgotten to write down.

Include a "List of numbers"—all kinds of important numbers: insurance policy numbers, Social Security numbers, bank account numbers and tax identification numbers for church shopping. This list has been a lifesaver on numerous occasions.

I had waited in a long line at the post office to secure Alan's passport for his trip to Germany. As Murphy's Law would have it, when I finally reached the desk, I was asked for the one document I did not have.

"No, ma'am. I don't have his Social Security card, but I do have his number here. Will that do?" "Sure," she replied. What a blessing!

I enjoy what I consider a ministry of loaning out books, tapes and other materials from my personal library, humble as it may be. But without my "Loaned-out list," I would not be so willing to share "my friends—my books" lest I lose them.

Make a "Gift list." It is so much fun to surprise and please others. When you hear someone you love very much, someone special, mention what he would like to have, jot down that

ORDER IN THE COURT

info on your "Gift list."

I overheard Mother telling someone that she'd like to have a set of those new molecular hair curlers. I wrote that on my "Gift list" and also on my "To buy" list. I was planning a trip to Sam's Club, where I found just what she wanted. When she came through Atlanta with Daddy, there was her wish come true sitting on the dining room table—brand new molecular curlers. And we set in right away to try them out. It is so much fun to surprise people you love.

No, no, I haven't forgotten myself. I like to keep a list of things I want, too. There are several reasons for this "Wish list." The obvious reason is to respond intelligently to my loved ones who want to lavish me with lovely gifts on birthdays and other special occasions.

But this black-and-white list helps me to see my desires and manage my wants, too. After I write it down and look at it awhile, I often decide, "I don't want that after all." Then there's no hassle of returning it. I am also convicted when my wants get "out of hand," if you know what I mean.

Other lists are: "Prayer list" and "Vacation packing list." You'll have others.

Business Cards: This section is a plastic, compartmentalized sheet for library cards, business cards, driver's license, insurance cards, wholesale membership cards, check cashing cards, etc.

Addresses and Phone Numbers: This section is not a complete listing but those addresses and phone numbers used most often.

Notepaper and Stamps: This section is a sealable pouch of notepaper, envelopes and stamps for letter writing. Oftentimes I find myself waiting—how about you? The waiting room is just one place where I wait. When Rick and I go to the hospital together, sometimes just one of us at a time is allowed to visit the patient. While waiting, I have the means to catch up on correspondence.

Turning to my "List" section, I see whom I need to write.

21

ORDER IN THE COURT

Opening the stationery pouch, I get out the supplies needed. The letter is written, sealed, addressed, stamped and dropped in the hospital letter-drop before leaving. It feels so good to "redeem the time" in such a profitable way.

Post-It notes by 3M are kept here, too. When we call on someone who is not home, we can leave a personal note along with a tract or church brochure. I also keep several maps to our home here to help direct guests.

Notes: Here is where sermon notes, quotes and thoughts from daily devotions are kept. When this section gets too bulky, it is filed away in the A to Z system, which we'll discuss later.

Wallet: This is simply a zippered leather pouch for money and receipts. On the other end of this "wallet pouch" is a small compartment where I keep extra keys to our house and cars. I am embarrassed to tell you just how many times these extra keys have kept us from calling a locksmith.

Supplies: My notebook already had spaces designed for pen and pencil and credit-card-sized calculator. I added a digital stick-on clock in the front of my notebook, too.

Photographs: This sentimental section holds pictures of my family. Having grown up in Atlanta and now serving the Lord here, I'm always running into old friends whom I haven't seen for a long time. They enjoy seeing the pictures of our family. Oftentimes you can catch me lovingly staring at my treasures, too.

Bible: Of course, I cannot put an entire Bible in my small notebook. But I did cut out the Psalms and Proverbs from an old Bible that was too worn to carry around. So even if I am caught without my Testament or Bible, I always have the Psalms and Proverbs with me.

Songs: Alan and I sing together, so I bring along the music to a few songs. If we are called upon to sing, we are prepared to serve the Lord through music.

Being in the midst of redecorating the den at this time, I also have swatches of fabric, trim and wallpaper tucked away in the cover sleeve. If I am interested in any particular item while out shopping, I can quickly see if it will match my decor without returning to the place of business bearing pillows or cushions.

I do hope that you will at least give the "notebook notion" a try. If you are like me, you'll find it very helpful. It will consolidate a lot of paper work; and you'll have everything in one place. It is "bound to be" a blessing.

CENTERS

You wouldn't like to shop in a department store where the Band-Aids were shelved with the dishwashing detergents, would you? Just imagine the frustration of shopping in a confusing setup like that. We can learn the value of establishing centers from the successful department store.

Store each item close to where you use it. The old adage is truly helpful: "A place for everything and everything in its place."

You cannot use what you cannot find. Daddy has done much reading and study on nutrition. He recently told me an interesting truth about the human body that is applicable here.

We are an organism. Of course, *organism* and *organize* have the same etymology. Our amazing human bodies can use organic minerals, but they cannot use inorganic minerals. The body, because it is an organism, that is, an organized living system, knows how to find and use "organic" or organized minerals. But since "inorganic" minerals are by their very name unorganized, our human organisms cannot find and use them. What an analogy!

When talking to Winnie the Pooh, Christopher Robin said, "Organizing is what you do before you do something, so that when you do it, it is not all mixed up."

We need to establish centers for various activities and

responsibilities, so we'll not be all mixed up. Again, your centers will differ from mine. Here are some suggested centers:

Home Office: You may quickly say, "Oh, I don't have room for that." Your home office need not be a desk and credenza with a bookshelf beside it. You could set up a simple home office in the corner of a room or even in a box. To manage a home efficiently, one should evoke all the skills involved in managing a business. Housekeeping is big business anyhow.

Business leaders take the following quote very seriously: "Quality is never an accident; it is always the result of intelligent effort." So let's work smarter, not necessarily harder. This home office will be the center of record keeping, "Accounts Payable" and general filing.

A to Z Filing System: Keep this general filing system in your home office. Here you will file such information as immunization records, correspondence, client copies of tax returns, warranties and instructions, paid and unpaid bills. The average home will not require any more elaborate filing than this simple A to Z system. If your family's functions include home education or telecommuting, then additional and specialized filing will be necessary.

Checkbook and Accounts: "Not slothful in business; fervent in spirit; serving the Lord" (Romans 12:11). This verse is in the front of our checkbook. Financial advisor Larry Burkett suggests only one spouse keep the checkbook. He advised that the spouse who has the time, interest and ability take on this project.

Since I was the bookkeeper for Curtis Hutson Revival Campaigns for several years, I had the experience and interest to fulfill this task. My husband is the overseer. I am the bookkeeper; he is the accountant.

We use a pegboard system for writing checks with a built-in dispersement journal. At the end of each month, Rick can clearly see how every penny was spent or invested. Come April 15, tax preparation is simplified since the expenses have been dispersed month by month.

Family Bulletin Board: Mount a small bulletin board in the most frequented area of your home for "in-house" messages and reminders. Ours is above the kitchen telephone. This is the "nerve center" of our home. I've already suggested you post a large family calendar in this same area; the bulletin board is an excellent place for that calendar. We use our church calendar with services and activities already printed on it. All events, games, music lessons, parties and appointments must be checked against that calendar, approved by Mom and Dad, and penciled in on that date. The family bulletin board and calendar will help coordinate the entire family's schedules. Unnecessary trips will be avoided, surprises will be minimal, and backtracking will be nil.

Addresses and Phone Numbers: Such information needs to be easily accessible and updated. The standard format address books are not the best. Adding, deleting and changing addresses or telephone numbers makes a messy directory. The information will eventually become illegible, and you will have to start all over again and redo the entire roster.

The most up-to-date and efficient method is the use of a personal computer. "Day-Timers" markets a software program for the storing and printing of addresses and phone numbers, with various extra ways of filing and tagging.

If this medium is not available to you, try this idea. A very simple, workable system is a 3 x 5 card file. This is how I kept a current directory for many years. Record one name, address and phone number per card. The card may also store other valuable information: children's names, relatives, birthdates, clothing sizes, maps or directions to their residence, baby's due date, prayer requests, etc. When a change occurs, your update is simply to redo one card. Pull it out of the file and replace it. This is much easier and tidier than a book filled with X's and a mind filled with ?'s—"Just which address is the current one?"

ORDER IN THE COURT

Implement some ideas from the telephone company. You've noticed how phone books are "chained" to the public telephones. Although you may have more than one copy of your personal telephone directory, make sure at least one copy is always available for use. Attach that one near your family bulletin board. Literally nail it down or chain it down. No more "Where's the phone book?"

When a family member needs to put in an entry or get information from the book, he must do it "on site." You will always know where the address book is.

Our addresses are divided into four sections: Family, friends, church roster and "yellow pages." If you relocate to another town, your personalized "yellow pages" and church roster will be obsolete sections; but your unchanging family and friends sections will remain absolute.

Keys: I've already made confession that keys have been a problem for us, so we've tried different ways to relieve ourselves from getting "all keyed up" over them. A key rack hangs near the family entrance to our home. My brother Tony gave me a message center with a bulletin board and dry-erase marker board that closes, concealing the keys and revealing a pretty picture. That's where our keys belong. But the simplest key rack, a cup hook, will work just as well. We've made it a habit of hanging the keys up "first thing" when we walk through the door.

When our baby Jana Kay came along, I was in need of an extra set of hands. I could not give up one of the hands I already had for the exclusive purpose of holding a keyring. You can understand. So I freed this "hand in demand" by putting my keys on a coil that I could wear around my wrist.

The only problem with this coil is the identification that comes along with it. When I am in the department store, people are always asking me where to find something. They think I am a sales associate with that key coil around my arm.

Still "keying in" on keys, reduce the number of keys you

must carry by use of a master key system for your home. Our Uncle Jim is a locksmith, and he recently re-keyed our locks. Now one key fits all—the doorknob and deadbolt locks.

If your deadbolts require a key to unlock, then keep one by each door. Place it on a hook where the children can reach it, so that in case of fire they can get out quickly. Store extra keys to your house and cars in a magnetic holder on the side of your refrigerator.

For seldom used keys, buy a key cabinet with numbered tagging from an office supply. Label each key and store the small cabinet in a low priority storage area. I put still another set of house and car keys there, too.

In your notebook, under "lists," record who has copies of your keys. I have given duplicate keys to our neighbor, a close friend, Daddy and others. Now if you really want a good motivation to keep your house in order at all times, just give your traveling evangelist, meticulous father a key to your house. Give him liberty to come and go at will, and you'll consistently have to keep your house ready and waiting. He is always traveling through Atlanta, and I'm thankful for the frequent opportunities we have to visit together.

Photograph Albums: This obsessive behavioral pattern of mine really needed some boundaries and management. Do I ever love pictures! Herein lies a real weakness. If this love is not managed somehow, I could easily spend all our money at the photographer's studio.

Limits were set when we decided to have one—and only one—family portrait taken each year. Every year since we were married, we've gone back to our award-winning photographer, David Smith of Smith Studio of Photography, who took our wedding pictures. On or near our wedding anniversary, he photographs a family sitting. Each and every year this family portrait is added to an old-fashioned leather and suede album. This beautiful collection is a record of the children's births and annual growth, as well as a record of our aging process. What an awful thing to have on record! On our

50th wedding anniversary, we should have quite a pictorial story to share, Lord willing.

But what about the thousands of snapshots? To simplify matters, keep an album on each child, each set of grandparents, each brother or sister's family, and an album for friends. File the pictures in chronological order. Your older children can help. Children love pictures, you know, especially those of themselves. When your children marry, you could present them with their own individual volumes.

A friend "crops" her snapshots, saving only the better parts of each print. So instead of inserting each 35mm print in a plastic sleeve, she creates a mural effect on larger 8-1/2-x-11-inch sheets. She loves pictures as much as I do, and this method saves her lots of space.

It doesn't matter what system you use, but do have a system of some kind. A date stamp saves lots of time when dating the backs of prints. I'd like to write a "cutesy caption" on the back of every one, but there is no time for that at this stage of my life. If I waited for that kind of time, there would be no albums to enjoy and share. Maybe someday I'll have time for that, and then I can enjoy reliving the memories.

You can get double prints for nearly the same cost of single prints. Take advantage of those special offers, and send pictures to family and friends. Everyone loves pictures, especially your loved ones who live distances away. Pictures will help fill in the gaps between visits.

Scrapbooks: Although my mind is a curator of memories with a special gallery for each dear person in my life, I cannot give you a guided tour through my mental museum. It is my own private collection; and, oh, how beautiful it is!

But if I am to share even a few of these treasures from time to time, I need scrapbooks to place in your hands and before your eyes. Use the same simple guidelines we discussed for cataloging photographs. Chronologically paste relics and reminders in scrapbooks.

On our honeymoon, I presented my husband with a

treasure box. During our engagement, I'd written more than two hundred preachers and leaders, asking for their advice on leadership and pastoring. The response was a blessing. Rick received unmatched advice from great preachers, many of whom are now with the Lord. I also asked the preachers to include their favorite sermon outline—what a treasury! He received sound suggestions from successful leaders such as our President and governor, too.

For many years, this information and inspiration lay hidden away in that box. There were so many letters and outlines; I was puzzled as to how I could organize the bulky material. A dear friend, Miss Ronnie Willis, helped me display each precious piece in a sheet protector and then in albums, volumes one and two. Now this rare treasure is out of its box and can be enjoyed by many.

Redecorating: Decorate with meaningful pieces, not just what is current fashion. There is a piece of art I'm saving my dollars to buy. It is an oil painting by Civil War artist Dick Lopeman called "The Preacher's Wife." A worn-out, hard-working preacher's wife is seen toting water back and forth, to and from the little church in the background where soldiers were in hiding.

My husband also has a favorite, given to him by a dear church member, Nancy McNeese. "A Preacher's Tools" by Ron Cockerham is a watercolor print, composed of a Bible and a concordance. Sitting atop the concordance is a pair of wing-tipped shoes and a pack of Halls cough drops.

Other painters feature religious art. I admire the scriptural works of our local artist Sandy Clough.

Another resident artist I enjoy is Anni Moller, who is known for her watercolors of metropolitan Atlanta's landmarks. These prints are meaningful memories for me, as I grew up in the suburbs of Atlanta.

Not every item in your home can, or really should, be a "top-of-the-line" product. There are more important ways to spend the money God gives us. But each room needs a quality focal point—a place where your eyes find rest, just because it is beautiful and meaningful. That focal point can be anything you choose.

Decorating ideas from magazines, newspapers and sales fliers can be filed in your A to Z system under "D." My ideas outgrew that file, so now I use a 3-ring notebook with pocket dividers. There is a divider for each room and area of the house. The articles and pictures are easily dropped in the pocket dividers. When changes are needed around the house, I go to this collection of ideas that have, for some reason, already made an impression on me.

Video and Cassette Tapes and Compact Discs: Specialty shops that carry organizing tools offer all sorts of equipment for storing these particular items. But the cost could be more than you want to pay.

Audio and video recordings are great entertainment and educational tools, but practice the principle of "elimination and concentration," and streamline your collection. These items take up much space. Make that up-front investment of time and discard all recordings you have not viewed or heard for a long time. Throw away those you do not plan to use any-time soon.

Here is an inexpensive way to store audio cassettes. Purchase shallow, under-the-bed particle board boxes with sliding door covers. The ones I bought were advertised as shoe storage. We mounted them on the wall with the bottom side against the wall and the sliding doors facing us. I hope you can visualize this verbal description. One revised "cabinet" is labeled "Music"; another, "Sermons"; another, "Children's Tapes"; and another, "Women's Messages." The solid doors cover the stacked cassettes, avoiding the look of clutter.

If you try this method, please reinforce the innovative "cabinet" with wooden corner molding underneath, before you put cassettes inside. When fully loaded, the boxes become very heavy and need that extra support to keep them from sagging along the bottom edge.

Cassettes can capture memories that are easily enjoyed by the entire family. One of my favorites is the video cassette I put on my "Want list" two Christmases ago. I asked Mother and Daddy to put their old 8mm home movies on VHS tape; and it was my best gift that holiday. I have the footage of Daddy baptizing me. I cry every time I see it. My parents took a lot of home movies. Guess I get that trait honestly, huh?

Games, Toys, Children's Books, Costumes and Hats: Centers need to be designated for each of these categories. Children's paraphernalia can permeate the entire palace if you don't watch it.

To reduce quickly the space required for storing games, try this suggestion. Copy or cut out game instructions and laminate them on the backs of the gameboards with clear contact paper. This takes very little time but saves lots of space. Discard the manufacturer's packaging—that is, the box—and reduce your three-foot stack of *game boxes* to a three-inch stack of *game boards*. Depending on the size of your collection, you can probably fit all of your newly consolidated games into just one shallow drawer.

Safely tuck all the illusory little game pieces into small baskets or tins that will also fit into your new game drawer. If you are like most folks, your space is at a premium. This tip will free up some of that sacred space.

Most of our games are downstairs in the playroom; that is where we play, put puzzles together, etc. There are no toys in the children's bedrooms. Remember that we are trying to store items where they are used; and the children sleep, not play, in their bedrooms. The boys' bedroom is shared by both of them, and the room is only big enough for their beds, a chest of drawers and a small desk with a chair. Jana Kay's bedroom has to double as a guest room sometimes, so there's no room for toys there either.

A few quick games are stored in the drawer of an end table in the living area, where we have family devotions. Many evenings we spontaneously pull out a quick, five- or ten-minute game just before devotions. The children love it. But if those games such as Uno, Boggle, Dominoes, Othello, Memory or Clever Endeavor were not within reach, we would not take the time to hunt them down.

Try buying toys that don't have too many pieces. One-piece toys are ideal, but not usually practical for children's "role playing" and imitations of real life situations. Toys with too many little pieces are hard to keep altogether. I try to steer away from that extra hassle, but Legos are the exception to that tidy rule. Our boys love their Legos.

As a motivation to put their toys away before "leaving the scene of the accident," we have what is called a "Redemption Box." I wish I could remember who shared this teaching tool with me; I would like to give credit to that innovator. It is not original with me, but we have used it with success. Let me explain how it works.

When toys are left out after play is finished, they end up in the "Redemption Box." If I am forced to come along behind them and pick up their toys, the children must "redeem" their toys by some action above and beyond their regular daily chores. This is a graphic reminder of the meaning of the word *redemption*, as we apply it in a spiritual way.

What about voluminous volumes of children's books? Little bitty books scattered everywhere can give a cluttered look. Children must learn to love books, and this can only be accomplished by fun exposure and experiences with them. So we want to refrain from negative comments like "Just look at these messy books." Here's a helpful hint.

Invest in a few sturdy vinyl magazine holders. You can order them through office supply catalogs or purchase them at office supply stores. Even very young children want to cooperate; but they need help, guidance and just the right tools. Our youngest child can stuff all her little books into a wide magazine holder and shelve it herself. When she is finished, the books are neatly hidden away on the bookshelf where they belong. As we often say around our house, "Now, that'll work." Then when she wants to "read," she knows where her books are.

The children have a box of costumes and a box of hats, and we rummage through those boxes more often than you'd think. We choose not to celebrate Halloween, but the church AWANA program offers an annual Fall Festival, where the children are allowed to dress in costume if they wish. Children love to play "dress up." Give them this gift, a box of costumes, to stimulate their imaginations.

Gift Wrapping: Keep it simple. A small plastic trash can will adequately hold rolls and sheets of wrapping paper. And an attached plastic bag will hold the bows and ribbon. I use a drawer in an old dresser down in the basement. Here I keep paper (bought by the pound at a paper factory outlet), scissors, both transparent and cellophane tapes for different types of wrappings, ribbon, ribbon shredder (for special effects), gift tags, pen and tissue paper. These items are never "borrowed" from that drawer.

Purchase only a few paper patterns: one feminine, one masculine, one childish, and one all-occasion. You can use the newspaper comics to wrap some gifts. A cute idea for a baby shower is to wrap the gift in a baby blanket and attach with diaper pins.

Keep a roll of colored cellophane paper for hard-to-wrap and otherwise bulky gifts. Include plain white paper for any occasion. You can add a bow and small kitchen utensil or another novelty that would better fit the occasion. With gift-wrapping supplies on hand, you won't have to wrap a gift in the car on the way to the party, as I'm sure all of us have done at one time or another.

While gabbing about gifts, I include that it is helpful to keep miscellaneous ones in the closet to avoid that "emergency spending." My "generic" gift is a picture frame. I know what you're thinking, "How fitting, coming from Miss Shutter-bug herself!" A picture frame is appropriate for almost any occasion that includes a celebration, whether it be a wedding, graduation, birth or birthday. I buy picture frames anytime I catch them on sale. If I don't give them as gifts, I can certainly use them myself, right? Keeping a supply of standard gifts will save you time, money and mental anguish over what to buy.

Close friends and family don't usually receive picture frames from me on their special days. Remember, that "Gift list" I have will help me when shopping for those special loved ones.

Recipes: You can purchase specialty dividers to fit a 3 x 5 recipe file. Categories include: breads, casseroles, beverages, vegetables, salads, desserts, etc. One lady has only two categories: "Family favorites" and "Someday-I'll-try." Purchase some pretty recipe cards for sharing recipes with others.

Vital Records: Your "vital records vault" could be a safe deposit box at the bank. Or you could protect your vital records (wills, insurance policies, birth certificates, marriage licenses, jewelry appraisals, deeds and titles, etc.) in a home-style safe or fireproof box at home. If you choose to rent a safe deposit box at the bank, take this warning seriously: Be careful what you stash there and have a couple of people on the signature card besides husband and wife. In the event both spouses were taken to Heaven at the same time, the box would be sealed until court proceedings were concluded. Make a copy of everything in your safe deposit box. Keep the key to your box in that key cabinet of seldom used keys.

Mail: Incoming and Outgoing: Americans use fifty million tons of paper annually. The accumulation of paper in our homes is a real heavy-duty problem. We are all victims of the paper plague. Stand over the wastebasket when you open your mail and make decisions "on the spot," processing each piece only one time.

Bills and financial statements belong in your home office with your "Accounts Payable." Post all events you'd like to attend on the family calendar, discarding the actual invitations, fliers or advertisements. On the calendar make sure to include information such as the time, place, map and what you need to bring to the event. Go ahead and post *every* activity, even if you are not certain you can attend. Your schedule may be freed up so that you'll be able to attend after all.

What about all those bulky catalogs and magazines? How can we quiet the growl of this "Paper Tiger"? Throwing away perfectly good and resourceful magazines really used to bother me. But when I realized that the public library has copies of many magazines to which I subscribe, I breathed a sigh of relief. Through their "InfoTrac" network, I can find most any article I need. And this system cross-references hundreds, maybe thousands, of magazines and newspapers.

Refuse to let magazines and catalogs become refuse. Don't let them pile up. Clip out articles you want to read and put them in a folder labeled "To Read." Clip out advertisements of merchandise you wish to purchase and put those with your "Accounts Payable." You'll be reminded to place your order as you are writing checks. Throw away the rest of the magazine or catalog.

Set up a "letter drop" near the family exit, so you will see the letters and packages to be mailed on your way out the door. I use a wooden napkin holder that matches the decor of the kitchen. It sits on the counter we walk past on the way out.

Safety: Proper lighting is part of safety. Low-wattage, plug-in guide lights keep our path safe during the night hours. When the children were very small, I attached specially designed "pulls" on the switch plates so they could turn the lights on and off themselves with the colorful, beaded cords.

Keep a rechargeable flashlight plugged in each room, especially the bedrooms. Know where emergency candles and matches are. Keep your batteries together and in their original packaging (to know which ones are freshest). I've heard that batteries, like vitamins and other perishables, stay fresher and last longer when stored in the refrigerator.

Emergency telephone numbers are laminated near each phone in the house. In my and my husband's room, these numbers are laminated on the inside of the night stand drawer, but easy to find. In the boys' room, the emergency list of numbers is laminated with clear contact paper on the top of their desk, under the phone itself—again, out of sight until needed. Near the kitchen phone, the list is on the inside of the closest cabinet door.

The phone numbers on these lists include the local police station, fire department, closest hospital, poison control center, ambulance service, husband's and/or wife's office, neighbors on both sides, close friend and 911, which dispatches almost any type of emergency call.

When thrown into an emergency-type situation or when one becomes nervous and afraid, one's mind often goes blank. For this reason include your *own* name, address, phone number and general location (including names of main roads and landmarks) on that list of "Emergency Phone Numbers." When the dispatcher asks you for that information, you will be staring right at it, and you can just read it off the sheet. Dispatchers say many people forget their own names when they panic.

We had the local fireman come to our home and teach us fire safety. We learned so much. He left a video and written material with us for our continued learning. You might save the lives of your dear ones by taking the time to have your fireman come demonstrate.

Install smoke detectors in every room of your house. They are very inexpensive. Put in new batteries annually on some selected holiday or someone's birthday.

Sit down as a family and lay out a fire escape route, using a sketch of your home's floor plan. Decide in advance just what to do in case of a fire. The fireman demonstrated how a person has only a few minutes to get out of the house. There's not much time to think before dark smoke blinds and quickly suffocates.

Close all bedroom doors at night. If a fire should start while the family is asleep, the smoke detector will sound. Closed doors would protect those in that room from threatening fire. Teach the children to feel the door. If it is very warm, do not open it; fire would spread quickly into their rooms if opened. Teach them how to escape through a window. Keep a roll-up, lightweight ladder in those rooms too elevated to jump from. Or demonstrate to your children how they can use a simple belt to descend from an upper level.

As soon as the smoke alarm rings, loudly warn and awaken the family. According to preplans, each will begin his exit. Then dial 911 or the fire department. That emergency phone list will be a real lifesaver now.

Designate a "meeting place," where each member of the family will wait when they've escaped. This plan will make it clear when everyone is safely out of the house. Don't waste valuable time asking, "Is Johnny still in the house?" If Johnny is not at the "meeting place," he is still in the house, and the firemen will go after him. Our designated spot is the mailbox. Don't forget to keep keys by each door; there is no time now to be looking for keys.

Can you guess what is the number-one fire hazard in any home? I thought it would be the stove or oven or—an even better guess—the space heater. But I missed with all of those guesses. The television is the cause of most house fires. Well, that's just another good reason to keep the TV turned off. A television fire usually ignites hours after it has been turned off. And most dangerously, that's usually when the family is already in a deep sleep. As my sage father satirically stated this Shakespearean quote, "T-V or not T-V; that is the question."

Visit your local home improvement stores for even more safety devices, like motion sensitive lighting and outdoor guide lights. As soon as the price comes down, we plan to invest in radon detectors that notify when there are dangerous levels of radon in the air.

First-Aid Kit and Medicine Cabinet: Set up a medical center. A clear plastic covered box is ideal. Your local drug store can provide you with a complete listing of products that need to be kept on hand. Check the expiration dates on medicines and discard the deadly outdated ones. I like to get a fresh supply of first-aid products when our local drug store has its annual half-price sale on their already inexpensive store brands.

Here are some items that we keep in the first-aid center: gauze, tape and scissors, cotton balls, Band-Aids, hydrogen peroxide, witch hazel (for bruising), rubbing alcohol, Gold Bond powder, ankle wrap, arm sling, heating pad, ice packs, blood-pressure cuff, Epsom salts, antiseptic, topical antibiotic, boric acid (antifungal), camphor spirits, mentholatum (analgesic), Mercurochrome, milk of magnesia, Ipecac (to induce vomiting in case of poisoning), insect repellent, thermometer and your desired medications for fever and pain. Some products will need to be refrigerated. Your one-of-a-kind family will have specialized needs, too.

Keep your medical guides and pamphlets in this medical center. A good laymen's medical journal is *The Better Homes and Gardens Medical Book*. We recently added a book that Daddy recommended: *Prescription for Nutritional Healing* by James F. Balch, M.D., and Phyllis A. Balch, C.N.C.

Take a short course in first-aid and also learn CPR. Every mother loves her family enough to take the time to learn how to save their lives.

Travel Items: Designate an area for travel items. If you travel often, these items will need to be very accessible. If your lifestyle includes little travel, these seldom used items can be stored in "secondary" storage areas that we'll cover a little later.

Travel items include: suitcases, carry-on bags, garment bags, travel iron, maps, power converter and travel-size toiletries.

Stuffed Animals: What do you do with your children's colossal collection of cuddly critters—their stuffed animals? While our maturing Alan and Curt are ready to get rid of them, sentimental Mother is not. Here's a cute idea; and if I can do this, anyone can.

Make an "animal tree" from a wooden banister pole intended for porches. Purchase the unfinished pole from a hardware store and install it wherever the toys are located. If you are not afraid to use a drill, you can hollow out holes at different levels and on all sides of the pole. Then glue in pegs made from cheap wooden dowels. If this will not work for you, simply use cup hooks to position the fuzzy friends. Paint or stain the "tree" to match the room. Tie coordinating ribbons or just rubber bands around the necks of the animals for hanging. One lady told me she tried this idea, wedging sturdy carpet tubing between the ceiling and floor.

Add large tropical silk greenery to the top, and you have a very attractive and practical way to display your babies' first toys. The "animal tree" adds a lot of color to the playroom, too.

Our boys have quite a collection of "Matchbox" cars and "Micro-machines." They still enjoy them from time to time. But when they "grow out of them," I plan to display the collectibles in a way which we'll all enjoy for years to come.

You may want to try this idea, too. Buy one or two large, clear-glass lamp bases. You have probably seen such lamp bases filled with shells. But your functional display case will "bring to light" the tiny trucks and treasures that your tough tykes toyed with as toddlers.

Barbershop: I have always enjoyed barbering. Pawpaw Hutson was a barber, and Mawmaw Hutson was a beautician. So naturally as a high school student, I enjoyed working a part-time job at a nearby salon.

I hang out the "red and white barber pole" in the kitchen where the flooring is easier for cleanup. The "barber shop" center is a plastic dishpan that fits on an extra shelf we installed under the kitchen counter. The space was otherwise wasted.

In this makeshift barber shop, there are capes (small and large), combs, clips, thinning shears, cutting shears, clippers and attachments, spray bottle of water, travel-size hair dryer, loose-bristle brush for removing hair from neck and clothing, and powder. I still enjoy using some of my grandfather's old shears that are as good as new.

A real treat for me is cutting Daddy's hair when he travels through Atlanta. I love to cut his hair because that is one time I have him all to myself; we have good talks. I have his undivided attention; he doesn't move a muscle because he wants a good haircut.

Personal Toolbox: Your husband probably has a nice tool kit; so does mine. But it is not always available to me when I need it. It is too big for me anyway; so I got me a small, lightweight plastic one and stocked it with all the household hardware tools and equipment I need and use often.

Most repair jobs are left undone simply because it is too much trouble to get to the right tools for the job. Do you agree? This personal toolbox is kept in the laundry room in a most handy spot. Along with the toolbox sits a tiny compartmentalized bin for screws, nails, tacks, hooks, wire, picture hangers, etc.

A word of warning: Don't try to be a jack-of-all-trades. Get professional help when you need it. Don't continually say, "Well, I could do that myself." If that's true, then why haven't you already done it? You need not feel guilty if you can't do everything yourself. Some jobs can only be done by professionals. I speak from "failed experiences." Those experiences ended up costing us a lot more time and money because of mistakes and messes.

Music: This "pile up" was an unwieldy stack to compose. Both boys take piano and trumpet lessons. There is a congeries of choir arrangements, as well as wedding music,

ORDER IN THE COURT

solos, duets, trios, Christmas and Easter cantatas, various hymnals, the Favorites series, and Patch the Pirate sing-alongs. This collection of choral arrangements needed a cabinet of its own.

A repository sits beside the piano with enough room to store a small electric keyboard, recorders, flutes, harmonica, guitar picks and autoharp as well as the music. Hanging on the wall in between the cabinet and piano, in decorative fashion, are ukuleles. This is our consolidated music center.

Outdoor Attire: The amount of space imposed for coats, hats, gloves and umbrellas will depend on the climate in which you live. This allotment need not be an actual "coat closet." Use a coat rack at the entrance and exit of your house. I prefer the small type that mounts to the wall, over the standing type that takes up floor space.

Hairbows: Where can you hide a puffy, plump pile of pretty hairbows? You cannot squash them in a small box; they'll lose their shape. For years a padded-topped, empty basket sat on the bathroom floor—just for looks; while the bathroom drawers were bursting with barrettes and bows. No more!

Now the basket conceals the "billions of bows," with plenty of room for them to lie loose; and the bows are situated where they are used, too. Jana Kay has a smaller decorative basket of bows in her room. Her Aunt Kay, my baby sister, gave the beautiful basket (filled with flowers) to us after spending a week in our home—a sweet hostess gift. Jana Kay's bows fill the small basket, and the others are clipped around the handle—only adding to the beauty.

While you may not have need to form all the functional focuses already referred to, you will construct other centers unique to your own lifestyle and affairs.

CLUTTER-FREE

Clutter invades everyone's life sooner or later. Clutter is an accumulation of things that don't have a home. Get a load of this statistic. There are 300,000-plus items in the average home. Is your home above or below average? Just imagine if only a small percentage of these items were out of place. What kind of clutter would be produced?

The cost of clutter can be a real killer. Commercial storage space rents for about 10 to 13 cents per square foot. This is very cheap when compared to the cost of the floor space in your home. A very conservative estimate is $11.00 per square foot. Don't waste your valuable space on clutter.

Since some of us don't want the upkeep of a larger house, or cannot afford a more capacious one with more storage space, we must employ a system to keep clutter at a minimum so as to provide more spacious living area in our homes.

Eliminate and concentrate. This is a key phrase. *Eliminate* those things you don't use and don't need; *concentrate* on building and upgrading the quality of those things you use and need. Be ruthless when it comes to clutter. Don't ask, "Is it still useful?" It probably is. Instead ask, "Do *I* still use it?"

Be a giver. Give things away—right away. Don't wait until you die to give away china that you haven't used for years. And every unused garment in your closet can be worn by a less fortunate person. Friends, relatives and charities all appreciate a giving person far more than they do a pack rat.

Last November my husband and older son went on a missions trip to Romania. The two weeks they were out of the country, Curt, Jana Kay and I went to visit my folks. Mother had planned a garage sale, so I brought a few things to throw in along with hers.

The weather was cold and damp. We all got sick sitting outside the entire day. I'm not sure it was Mother's first garage sale, but I'm positive it was her last. It was so much trouble; we decided to give everything away from now on. I did make a little money, but on the way back home, the fuel pump on our van had to be replaced. The cost was more than the amount I made at the garage sale.

Use the "in and out" inventory rule. When your home reaches its saturation point, apply this rule: If something new comes in, then something old goes out. Apply this rule to everything from toys to clothes to books. Stick to it, and you'll always be in control of your clutter.

Avoid duplicates. It is easy to accumulate unnecessary duplicates, especially in the kitchen. If you need duplicate utensils, by all means, keep them. There is one particular kitchen utensil that I need duplicates of: the Kitchamajig. I use that thing for blending, mixing, beating, draining, straining and stirring. I just must have two of them. But I was able to give away most of my other duplicates.

Junk drawers have purposes. Indulge in one junk drawer per person in the family. Select a small drawer, where items, yet without a home, can be "fostered" until a suitable home can be found. The drawer needs to be small enough so that you can't accrue too many items with which you know not what to do.

My husband's junk drawer is the place where he empties his pockets. Provide your husband with such a place. If an exclusive drawer is not available, give him a decorative stationery box with a lid. Set it conveniently on the chest of drawers where he changes. My husband once used the tray on his valet, but it was too small. And it was not covered storage, giving the appearance of clutter.

Speaking of the appearance of clutter, you can avoid unsightly cords with nifty devices that wrap the creepy coils in hidden canisters.

Clutter has been dubbed the biggest time-waster in housekeeping. So pick up clutter and train your family, also.

CLEANING

Everything, and I mean everything, needs cleaning, doesn't it? Seems though I'm always cleaning something—the house, the car, the children, the clothes, the yard, me, my hair! What do you think is the dirtiest spot in your house? Professional commercial cleaner Don Aslett said that doorknobs are. When did you last clean yours? A vacuum cleaner salesman told me the mattress is the dirtiest spot in the house. He suggested shampooing them occasionally.

Preventive Maintenance: What can we do to help keep dirt out of the house? What up-front efforts will really "pay off" later?

First, install effective matting. Doormats placed inside and outside the doorway keep a lot of dirt out of the house. Someone said, "I don't like to use doormats. They are nothing but dirt collectors." Well, if I'm not mistaken, that's the point. I've read that doormats reduce the amount of dirt coming into your house by 75%. The first choice is an industrial type with rubber backing. Carpet samples are too small; and "throw rugs can really throw you."

Hotel Setup: One can learn a lot by examining a hotel setup. The accommodations are designed to conserve space and the man-hours required for maintenance. Wall lamps are mounted to keep the floors free of clutter and therefore easier to vacuum. Apply this principle by mounting your mop, broom and dustpan on the wall. Wallmount your ironing board and vacuum cleaner attachments.

Applying this principle a different way, I had a drop-leaf table installed in the laundry room. It provides lots of countertop space for folding clothes; but it can be easily folded when the laundry is finished. (Did I say, "Finished"? Is laundry ever finished? Not very often at my house.) With the extra counter space, I can confine the unsightly, dust-enhancing laundry patrol to just one private area. No more sorting and folding clothes in the living areas where laundry in its various stages creates an incredible look of clutter. Do you agree?

Heating and Air-Conditioning Filters: Every time Mother comes to our house she asks, "When was the last time you cleaned your filters?" She is such a good mommy. "Have you had your furnace checked out lately?" she asks.

How well I remember the time her conscientiousness literally saved our lives! When Jana Kay was born, Mother came to help me, as she always does when her grandchildren make their debut. She was so concerned because we used a space heater in the basement, and we spend quite a bit of time down there. She insisted I have the gas company come out for a preventative checkup; and it was a good thing she persisted.

As I was telling you, Jana Kay was just born, so we'd been inside for about two weeks. We had a potentially deadly gas leak, but we'd become accustomed to the light fumes, although looking back, we recalled unexplained headaches that were caused by the leak. Then we remembered that our guests, who came to see our new baby and bring in food, had commented about smelling something.

We finally called the gas company, who arrived shortly thereafter. We had a bad leak. The man was surprised that we'd not already had a serious explosion and fire. Someday you may be as thankful as we were for practicing regular preventive maintenance on potentially dangerous equipment.

Oriental Custom: You guessed it. Taking off your shoes before entering your home will keep out even more dirt and germs, too. Our precious pediatrician, Dr. Leila Denmark, 97 years old now, strongly suggests (as only she can) that shoes be removed inside the house, especially if you have carpeting. Steering away from a sickening saga, I'll simply ask you to think about all the different places the soles of your shoes trod on any given day. Imagine imbedding that gamut of germs in the carpeting where your toddlers and crawlers play.

The color selection of your carpeting and other flooring can cut down on the maintenance, too. We have red clay here in Georgia; white carpet is a poor selection. A little visible lint on a darker carpet is easier to clean than red clay on a white carpet.

Save yourself a little extra time by using fewer covers and coverlets on your bedding. The fewer items to arrange, the easier the bed is to make, especially for the children.

Strategy: Where do you start cleaning? This will depend somewhat on your personality. But experts say to begin with the areas that clean up the fastest so you can quickly see some accomplishment. When you can enjoy even the slightest improvement, you will be encouraged to continue on.

Then, at some point, start alternating with the more difficult and slower tasks. (Are we using psychology on ourselves? Maybe it'll help.) But don't save the worst until the last because you will have no energy left. One resource recommends starting in the living room and front bath where guests are likely to go.

Timing: When do you clean? Clean when you feel fresh and well. This is usually in the morning. Someone said, "An ounce of morning is worth a pound of afternoon."

Clean a little each day, especially if you have small children. I learned a great lesson from my piano teacher, Mrs. Dorothy Jacquot. She challenged me to make use of small time segments for practicing several times a day, instead of one-hour sittings. She realized back then that most of us don't have the luxury of long spans of time at our disposal. Thanks to her, today I am still conserving time by grabbing every five- or ten-minute segment I can. If you have small children, this is especially helpful. There seems to be very little, if any, time that is not consumed with caring for your little angels.

Ladies who have to work outside their homes Monday through Friday usually do more cleaning on Saturday. But the more small jobs you can eliminate during the week, even the slightest of chores, will leave more family fun time on that special weekend off.

We visited Biltmore Estates several years ago. In a mansion of that size, several people are employed full-time to clean. Of course, none of our homes require that kind of extensive maintenance, but we can certainly learn from this principle. Enjoy cleaning a little bit each day.

Clean when the mess is fresh. You've heard dirt broken down into these categories: Clean dirt and dirty dirt. Clean dirt is the children's toys on the floor. Dirty dirt is the dried-on spaghetti from last Friday night's supper. It is easier to clean "clean dirt" than it is to clean "dirty dirt." Make it easier on yourself: clean while the mess is fresh.

Clean when you expect the least amount of interruptions. Somehow we get in a rhythm that is beneficial. You don't want to break that positive pattern if possible.

Choose fall cleaning over spring cleaning. Think about the practicality of fall cleaning. With a fresh fall cleaning, your home is ready for the festive holidays when you usually have the most company. In the fall, the house will stay cleaner longer because there is less activity in the cooler months. In the spring, windows are opened, letting in dust and pollen where you've worked so hard; and there is more traffic in the spring and summer, too. Spring is the ideal time for family activities. Don't miss out on all the fun. Clean in the fall, and get the maximum benefits out of cleaning.

Set aside particular times for occasional cleaning events and post them on your calendar. If a request is made of you that can be deferred, honestly say, "I have an appointment I must keep." Then those occasional chores like shampooing the rugs, cleaning out the fireplace or waxing the floors, will not be derailed.

Enforce a self-imposed deadline when simple morning chores will be completed. Pinpoint that reasonable time of day when you wish to be free from household chores and ready for other important and fulfilling projects. Before this deadline (10:00 is reasonable for me), take a five-minute pickup in each room. If you're like me, you'll have to discipline yourself not to be distracted by other jobs you see undone. You cannot stop to do deep cleaning; this is just a quick pickup.

We have an expression we use at our house. I will say, "Take ten." In the military services this means ten minutes at ease; but at our house it means ten minutes of hard labor. Every family member except the baby gets busy for ten minutes of picking up the clutter. With the four of us (lacking Jana Kay, whose mess we are all cleaning up), working for ten minutes each, forty minutes of work gets done, and order is quickly restored.

Equipment: In any profession, having and using the right tools is important. And every trade requires its own unique tools. Keep this simple and inexpensive, as you don't need that many tools.

However, a good vacuum cleaner is a must. Make this investment whenever possible. Get a commercial style with an extra long cord. You'll save time if you're not continually plugging and unplugging.

One item you may not have on your priority list is a wet-dry vac or a shop vac. This is a most helpful and inexpensive piece of equipment. You'll use the wet-dry vac for dirty jobs like the fireplace. I wouldn't want to use an expensive sweeper for removing fine ashes that will ruin the filtering system in the vacuum. The wet-vac can be used for getting up spills and water leaks, too.

Renting seldom used equipment is preferable to buying. Renting is cheaper than buying, storing and maintaining such equipment as waxers and shampooers.

You can save money by making purchases at janitorial supply companies. Use economic concentrate cleaning supplies and add your own cheap water. Your basic supplies include: disinfectant, ammonia-type cleaner, window cleaner, degreaser and spray bottles.

We usually have too much equipment and supplies. Our cabinets are stuffed with stuff we never use. We end up using the same products over and over, don't we? Keep a small basket of supplies under the sink in each bathroom. That saves many steps running back and forth to get equipment and supplies.

One extra product you may like to use is for silk plants. A florist told me that most silks will hold up if washed with water. But some of the glues used to assemble them disintegrate in water. You can test yours. Silk-Renew is a product especially formulated for silks.

Don Aslett recommends a squeegee for the showers and windows. Cut down on the multiplying mildew by wiping down the shower tiles with the squeegee. This inexpensive piece of equipment is the only way to clean windows; but do purchase a professional one.

A lamb's wool duster with an extendable handle reaches all corners, ceilings and fans. A Massolin-treated cloth is good for dusting, and a dry sponge cleans and absorbs dirt from wallpaper.

Wear the right clothes when you are cleaning. A smock with big pockets is handy for temporarily pocketing items you find out of place. Whatever you choose, don't wear pajamas and a housecoat while cleaning. Bedclothes do not put you in the right mode for cleaning. These loose clothes also present danger. The fireman who came to our home told us that many fires are started because of loose, hanging clothes catching fire over the stove. Loose clothes lead to tripping and stumbling, also. One lady I read about wears a white uniform. She declares it puts her in the right mood for cleaning.

Bonnie McCollough, who wrote *Totally Organized*, emphasizes wearing the right shoes. Slippers cause the same effect as pajamas. Instead, she wears tennis shoes or running shoes. This puts her "on the right track." A friend told me that she changes shoes from time to time on an especially long day. The variance of pressure on her feet brings relief along the way.

COMMUNICATION

Hebrews 13:16 says, "But to do good and to communicate

ORDER IN THE COURT

forget not: for with such sacrifices God is well pleased."

Telephone: A cordless phone or even a phone with a long cord will free you to move around and do chores or keep a watch on young children while you are talking. Mine always seemed to get in the most trouble when I was preoccupied on the telephone. They knew I was "tied up" and couldn't follow them when I was busy talking. I'll never forget the astonished look on little Curt's face when I followed him into the bathroom on our new cordless phone. He was playing in the toilet and thought I was unable to get to him. Surprise!

Conscientiously limit the length of your telephone conversations. Give the caller your full and undivided attention for an allotted time, but then firmly and kindly say, "Good-bye." Too much time on the telephone gives opportunity for gossip. Matthew 5:37 admonishes to "let your communication be, Yea, yea; Nay, nay: for whatsoever is more than these cometh of evil."

When making a long distance call, have before you a list of subjects you need to discuss so you won't forget and waste time and money trying to recall the specifics you needed to relay.

I like to keep a church bulletin near the phone for several reasons. One reason is the prayer list; I can pray for missionaries and the sick among our church family when I am put "on hold." Then upcoming events are posted in the bulletin, and some phone calls are concerning the details of those events.

Teach your children telephone etiquette. They can be a real help to you and a blessing to your callers. We've taught the children to answer this way, "Hello, Camperson residence. This is Alan speaking. May I help you?" Teach them how you want messages taken, and keep paper and pencil by the telephone. (Ours is mounted on the wall beside the phone upstairs.)

I appreciate the way our children practice telephone manners. Many callers have made sweet comments about, not

50

only their choice of words, but their hospitable attitudes that transcend the telephone wires. One lady said, "I felt like I received a warm welcome just by the spirit I sensed in your son's voice."

We have scriptural prompters laminated on the handles of the telephones. "A word fitly spoken is like apples of gold in pictures of silver" (Proverbs 25:11). When one reaches for another receiver, these words are visible, "A man hath joy by the answer of his mouth: and a word spoken in due season, how good is it!" (Proverbs 15:23).

Birthdays and Anniversaries: These special days are God-given opportunities to communicate your love for others. Buy economical boxed cards. This is one case in point where it truly is the thought that counts, not the price of the card. To conserve space, I take the cards out of their boxes and file them in baskets under "Women," "Men," "Children," "Family" and "Special." This idea will work for "Get Well" wishes, "Anniversaries" and acknowledging "Congratulations," as well. I really enjoy contacting friends and family to celebrate their special occasions and share their joy.

You will need a month-at-a-glance calendar to be used exclusively for this purpose. (This information is not on my notebook calendar.) Use the calendar on a personal computer or a loose-leaf type. Post all the birthdays and other occasions you wish to acknowledge. I prefer the Administrator month-at-a-glance, loose-leaf notebook. It is always kept in the communication center with greeting cards and stationery.

A successful system is to write out all your greetings at the beginning of each month. Address the envelopes and pencil in the mailing date just above the stamp. Put them in the front flap of your notebook/organizer. You will be reminded to mail them, and they will arrive on time.

If this sounds planned, well, it is. Thoughtfulness is "thinkfulness." But you will have to be thoughtful on purpose. Where there is a will, there is a way.

Letter Writing: People who write the most interesting

and effective letters never answer letters; they answer people. Do you know what I mean? This earthly life is all about people—wonderful people.

Keep stationery with greeting cards, and don't forget that pouch of paper in your notebook for letter writing when you are waiting or have just a few extra minutes amidst your busy day. I had to learn to write notes instead of books, though. In the area of letter writing, we tend to judge others by their performances and ourselves by our good intentions.

Beethoven said, "I write you letters by the thousands in my thoughts." But that's not good enough. Everyone loves to get letters.

Holiday Greetings: Holidays are appropriate times to make meaningful contacts with others, especially out-of-town loved ones. We have sent a wide variety of holiday greetings on a wide variety of holidays. The most popular tradition is the exchanging of Christmas cards.

But to relieve some of the stress of the Christmas season, we send greetings on holidays that are otherwise overlooked. I especially like to greet friends and family on Thanksgiving, sharing my gratitude to the Lord for each one. We've also sent a specific New Year greeting, which can be sent anytime in the month of January, asking for prayer to see specific goals realized. One year we sent Valentines to those on our card list, expressing our love to each. Another year I borrowed an idea my sister Donna learned from her friend.

We did not send Christmas cards that particular year. But each card we received went in a tray that we kept where we have family devotions. Daily we chose one family's card to focus our prayers on for the day. I printed up a letter explaining what we had done and enclosed it in a "Thinking-of-you" card.

Some of my favorite cards are color copies of Alan's acrylic artwork. Often we enclose a family snapshot, too.

Our holiday card list is very extensive, so I cannot give up the time nor money each and every year. We select one holiday every other year to contact loved ones through greeting cards.

When you receive greetings, quickly update your address file with corrections and changes of addresses.

CLOSETS AND STORAGE

There are three basic kinds of storage. Primary storage is for your clothes and cosmetics—those necessities you use daily. Primary storage also includes your most readily available kitchen cabinets.

Secondary storage holds off-season clothes and items you use sometimes, like the ice-cream freezer or canning equipment. Dead storage houses your last five years of financial records and those other least called for items.

You can create extra storage space in many different places. Instead of attaching a short dust ruffle around the baby crib, make one that goes all the way to the floor. This additional storage is a good place to put away bulky baby equipment and new clothes the baby hasn't grown into yet. The clothes are not too far out of sight. That's a good idea because the baby will grow quickly; and how many times our own babies have outgrown their clothes, literally, before even trying them on! This secondary storage space is very convenient.

Do your closets have ample, empty space near the ceilings? For a very reasonable cost, you can buy ventilated shelving and add a lot of secondary storage space to every one of your closets. Now all of my closets have a little more "breathing" room. My husband has learned a sure way to make me happy—buy a shelf and put it up.

Give your kitchen cabinets that same kind of expansion. Our carpenter added an extra shallow shelf in each cabinet. The extra shelves are ideal for dishes and shallow bowls.

Our growing family needed even more storage space in the kitchen, so the carpenter designed a built-in booth for the eating area. Besides being very attractive, the new seating arrangement made it possible for the whole family, along with several guests, to sit down to meals together. The seats lift up to reveal a shipload of stowage, which I use to put away my largest and least used pots and pans. This newly formed storage space is a most convenient spot for table linens, and the step stool just fits there, too.

Jana Kay needed a bigger bedroom. Her room needed to lodge her baby crib, chest of drawers, changing table, rocker and rocking footstool, large daybed and two large end tables. Following the suggestion of a creative friend, we enlarged the room and added a few square feet simply by "gutting" the closet.

Renovations included adding that extra shelf in the top of the closet and covering both top shelves with decorative curtains on a long spring rod. All the small unsightly baby supplies are neatly tucked away, out of sight, behind that curtain. Jana Kay's changing table fit nicely inside the closet after half of the clothes bar was removed. I didn't need that much room for the tiny hanging garments; and removing the bar also gave me plenty of room to stand and dress her. Baby clothes are short, so the hamper and trash can fit on the floor under the reduced clothes bar.

Mounted on the wall over the changing table is a pretty white wicker shelf that matches the trash can. The shelf holds her own toiletries. Hung on the narrow side of the wall is a shoe rack, designed for infant's shoes. Under the standard wooden shelf, I mounted a large mirror. It isn't visible to anyone except Jana Kay. But while I'm tending to her, she can see herself in the mirror overhead. The movement in the mirror keeps her entertained during the process of diapering and changing clothes, when babies tend to be fussy.

This adaptation is a most commodious and practical setup for a nursery. All of the "baby clutter" can be concealed when the closet doors are closed, so the nursery always exhibits a neat appearance.

ORDER IN THE COURT

The nursery example illustrates the differences between "open shelving" and "covered shelving." Open shelving can also be called decorative shelving. An example of useful but open shelving is one we put over our dining room window. It serves as a cornice with lightweight embroidered curtains hanging from it while displaying dishes that match the wallpaper. Eye appeal and balance are major considerations in such arrangements.

When open shelving is used for storage, it gives the appearance of clutter, even if items are in their proper places. On the other hand, covered shelving always gives the appearance of neatness. When the choice is yours, go for the covered shelving every time.

Afford yourself additional storage space by selecting furniture that is both decorative and multi-functional. Instead of buying a beautiful bench (with no hidden storage) for the foot of your bed, restore an old footlocker. A charming antique chest hides stacks of sweaters and looks lovely at the footboard. My sister's antique chest serves as a coffee table as well as extra covered storage.

Consider beauty *and* function when buying furniture. It is just as unnecessary to spend excess money on accessories that are designed only for function, void of artistic or aesthetic qualities, as it is to purchase items for their aesthetic value alone. A pretty "pie safe" provides plenty of cabinet space. Use your family heirlooms for practical purposes like storing VHS cassettes instead of buying one of those utilitarian-styled boxes.

Your attic and basement are major areas for secondary and dead storage. These areas are usually out of sight, so use plain boxes or bins. I usually use utilitarian, uniform boxes. Using sturdy boxes of the same size and shape makes the job of stacking easier.

Here's a helpful hint that some people will never try, but they will be the losers. Number the boxes on all sides with a wide-tipped marker. Make up a coordinating 3 x 5 card for each box.

We've mentioned 3 x 5 cards several times already. No, I really don't have small 3 x 5 boxes sitting everywhere. I use one longer box; it is safekeeping for addresses, recipes and these storage cards we'll explain.

Each 3 x 5 card will store this information: box number, location, that is, basement, attic, crawl space, tool shed, etc., and a listing of items in that particular box. (Now I've really overdone it, huh? You thought I was crazy, and now you're sure I am!)

Let me reiterate that this is an up-front investment of time that will save you hours as the years pass by. And the initial process is not too terribly time-consuming either. However, I do suggest that you finish a thorough job of de-cluttering your home before starting this project.

I implemented this system twelve years ago and two long-distance moves ago. Systematic storage is very successful, and it made the relocations easier, too. And if you ever decide, out of desperation (the only way we do some things, you know), to try anything, including this "preposterous" notion, you'll need to do it only one time.

When you discard any item, just strike it off the card. And don't rewrite the cards; yours are the only eyes that'll see them. Adding items is just as simple. Then anytime the family makes spur-of-the-moment plans to go picnicking, just look in your 3 x 5 card file to find which box that picnic tablecloth is in. It sure beats a midsummer crawl through the attic in a 100-degree sweltering sauna. This system makes it quick and easy to find seldom used objects.

There are several persuasive testimonials I could insert here of hopeless homemakers who thought this storage card idea was ridiculous. But after trying it, they were sold. I hope you'll be another delighted doubter-turned-believer.

Couldn't we all use more storage space? Ask the Lord for wisdom and creativity to make the best use of what you have. He will help you; He wants you to be a successful homemaker. ". . .cease from thine own wisdom" (Proverbs 23:4). "If any of you lack wisdom, let him ask of God, that giveth to all men liberally, and upbraideth not; and it shall be given him" (James 1:5).

The following illustration may sound like a silly idea, but it just shows how there are so many ways to conserve space. One lady detested the sight of the toilet plunger poised beside the toilet seat. She tried to hide it every way she could. *There just must be a way,* she thought. Then the question came to mind, *Is there anything sacred about that long handle?* Of course not, so she cut the handle in half, making the plunger fit nicely under the sink, completely out of sight.

Your closets can have concinnity and color. Use colorful plastic hangers and coordinating baskets for socks, ties, belts or small shoes. You might cover the wooden rods with color-coordinating shower rod covers. You can find these at linen specialty shops. Now the plastic hangers will glide easily across the plastic-covered rod.

COOKING AND NUTRITION

The patterns we learned about establishing centers for a vast variety of other activities are good guidelines in the kitchen, too. Set up centers for food preparation, baking and cleanup. Designate a place for paper products and a tea/coffee center where coffeepot, mugs, creamer and sugar are all together. You may need a bread-making center and various others.

Food and the preparation of it is the axis around which much family activity revolves. There is nothing more welcoming than the smell of fresh food cooking and cooling. "The way to a man's heart is through his stomach." How true! I can just hear one of my college psychology professors, Dr. Walter Fremont, saying, "Lady, feed the brute!"

Prepare foods that your family likes. Meals can be both nutritious and tasty. Our younger son Curt made my day when he was about five years old. One of his favorites is homemade vegetable soup, and it's my joy to make it just for him. He stands over that big boiling pot with longing in his big, brown eyes; I can see his mouth watering.

One evening we were enjoying "Curt's soup" and cornbread. He said, "Mom, I know you won't be doing the cooking in Heaven, so will you tell Jesus how to make this vegetable soup?" Don't children have a way of melting one's heart?

Mrs. J. R. Faulkner was interviewed by the *Joyful Woman* magazine several years ago. I was impressed by her response to this question, "What would you do differently if you could go back and relive your life?" Mrs. Faulkner, mother of five sons, replied, "I would go to more of the boys' ball games and cook more of their favorite foods." Join me in taking that admonition to heart.

Serve a variety of foods that are not only nutritional and delicious, but eye-appealing, too. You can be more artistic than say, white chicken, white cauliflower, white mashed potatoes and white rolls. Yes, set a pretty table for the favorite folks in your life—your family. Don't spare any detail that will say to them, "You are special to me." Use only your very best for the very best, because that they are.

Learn what you can about good nutrition. Nutritional information has increased greatly, and what once was the famous "four basic food groups" has been changed to the new "food pyramid." This "pyramid" suggests we eat mostly grains and breads (the lower and larger portion of the triangle), next, plenty of vegetables and fruits, then, less meat and poultry products and the least consumption of fats (at the smallest apex of the pyramid).

By 10:00 o'clock in the morning, know what you're having for supper that evening. This may be a meal you'll prepare at home, a take-out dinner you plan to bring in, or supper out at a restaurant or in the home of friends. This doesn't mean you must start cooking at 10:00 a.m. But by making dinner plans early in the day, you can make much progress on the meal before that busy dinner hour arrives. Casseroles can be put together, salads can be finished, and vegetables pared and potted. Then last-minute preparations will be much easier.

Take some of the decision-making out of meal-planning by simply rotating your favorite menus. Remember the nineteen menus my mother made up; that's nearly three weeks without a repeat. My sister has the same dinner each Sunday. She's prepared it so many times, she has it "down to a science."

If your family's schedule is suitable, have your larger meal in the middle of the day. We're home-educating our children, so this is a possible and preferable choice for us. There are many benefits, including more time for family fun in the evenings.

Position frequently used utensils in a handy location. Mine are in a decorative pitcher on the counter of the preparation center. The drawer was too full, so this arrangement allows for more room there.

Save money shopping at a wholesale membership club, farmers' market or Co-op, and buy in bulk. Chest freezers can be bought at reasonable costs, making it more feasible and practical to purchase in volume. Keep your pantry stocked with staple items, sparing frequent trips to the grocery store.

Once in awhile, go on a cooking spree. It is just as easy to make two meat loaves as it is to make one. Have one for dinner and freeze the other one. Go ahead and make enough spaghetti sauce for two meals while you're at it. Save the extra entrees until later. Or carry them to someone recovering from sickness or to a new neighbor.

When taking food to the sick or to a new mother, be even more considerate by taking the meal in disposable, aluminum pans. A friend of mine, Mary Johnson, buys plates and bowls at garage sales for pennies, just for this purpose. She posts a note with the meal, letting the receiver know she doesn't have to bother returning the dishes. How kind and thoughtful!

A missionary daughter, Mimi Wilson, in her book, *Once a*

ORDER IN THE COURT

Month Cooking, carried this cooking spree idea to an exciting extreme. Mimi was inspired by her mother who always had good food to serve her guests (out in the middle of nowhere, mind you). She coauthored a book of detailed instructions on how to cook only once a month and have good food every meal.

Along this same line, the ladies' fellowship of our church is putting together our own such recipe book, using our favorite freezable foods. We plan to distribute the *Care-Free Cooking-Spree Cookbook* as a hospitality gift to each lady who visits the church.

Cooking is fun, but now we must finish the job. Kitchen cleanup is usually the only drawback to this rewarding job of culinary concoctions. But help yourself out by keeping a sink full of warm, soapy water so you can clean as you go along. Use a footstool in the kitchen for propping up one foot. This relieves pressure on the back when you must stand in one spot for a lengthy time.

CLOTHING AND LAUNDRY

We work better in pleasant surroundings, don't we? Since women have to spend a lot of time in the laundry room, it's worth a little "spiffying up." We recently redecorated the laundry room—crisp striped wallpaper, blinds and balloon valances, and under-the-counter florescent lighting. Along with an attractive appliquéd rack for hanging clothes, there are other decorations on the walls. The dreaded laundry room is not so dreadful anymore. Working conditions have improved. The atmosphere is especially delightful when the early morning sun and fresh morning air infiltrate the slightly raised window.

The frequency of this task depends on the specifics of your family. The average woman needs to process one load a day. Discarding all clothes hampers may be helpful. The "gathering" step of the laundering process will automatically be eliminated.

Each member of the Camperson clan takes his or her own soiled clothes directly to the laundry room. The dirty clothes are sorted right then and there into one of three clearly labeled clothes baskets: whites, darks, towels. (Use a permanent marker for labeling). If you have room, another basket might be labeled: delicates.

Detergents, bleaches, stain removers, fabric softeners, netted bags for delicates and hangers are in the cabinets over the washer and dryer. A plastic dishpan is there for soaking heavily soiled items. Salt and vinegar are there, too, for pre-washing colored clothing. This salt-vinegar rinse keeps dark or bright colors from fading.

Locate a copy of *The Stain Buster's Bible,* and keep it in the cabinet also. One of my latest "finds" was in the automotive department. "Goop," a degreaser designed to clean mechanics' hands, takes out many stains. Wisk is good on rust, and hair spray removes ink stains. This I've never tried, but a friend tells me that carburetor cleaner gets out what other formulas can't.

When the buzzer sounds, take those permanent press garments out of the dryer immediately. Hang them on the wall rack to spare the "touch-up" or ironing process. All laundry folds easier when tackled swiftly.

Here's a neat notion for storing and stacking sheets. Arrange them so the folded fitted sheet and pillowcases are concealed by wrapping the folded flat sheet around them. Can you picture that? The "benefit of this package" is that, when you change bed linens, you won't be searching for matching sheets and pillowcases. When you grab hold of the "package," the sheet ensemble will already be assembled. If you have no linen closet, sheets can be stored between the mattress and boxspring.

A last word about laundry. I saw a retractable clothesline over the bathtub in a hotel. The nifty novelty provided us with a place to dry clothing. Years later when this item became available in common department stores, I purchased one; it mounts on the bathroom tile. How convenient it is for drying lightweight baby clothes and other delicate clothing! The water drips right into the tub—no mess.

CHERISHED ITEMS AND KEEPSAKES

How many treasures you can keep depends on how much space you have and how creative you are in making them functional or decorative.

Keep token items only. A written journal is a meaningful way to record memories. The memory is what's important, not the actual items themselves. Expressing memories through your own written words can capture feeling and emotion that may dissipate through the years.

We have a book we call *Eben-ezer Stones* (I Samuel 7:12)—a padded, embellished photo album where answered prayers, miraculous provisions, personal notes, cards and keepsakes are preserved. While I don't have space to save all the sweet cards, I do save the special handwritten messages by clipping them from the cards.

If some special keepsake is just too massy or messy to keep, take a picture of it. (What else is new, right?) Put the snapshot in your *Eben-ezer Stones* book. Your cherished item is documented permanently. "Remove not the old landmark" (Proverbs 23:10).

Most mothers have a hard time discarding their children's keepsakes. Confession time again: every crumpled piece of artwork is a rare treasure to "Sentimental Sherry." I had to "get a grip" on this grandiosity.

We had to limit the souvenirs we saved. Each child now has a fairly large Rubbermaid box in his room with his name on it. But this box limits what we can keep. We go through it periodically, just for fun, but end up throwing away some things that lost their emotional pull.

Use your heirlooms whenever and wherever you can. The

thick-glassed, heavy antique barbicide canister that my grandfather used for many years in his shop is used to hold pens and pencils. As it's used daily, we think of him. Our grandfather was very talented. He made a small barber cabinet for his razors; it is an exquisite work of craftsmanship and most valuable to me. It is displayed by the telephone downstairs, holding notepads for taking phone messages.

The boys' boots are bronzed. One sits on the hearth and is useful for holding fireplace matches. Our Curt is named for his grandfathers, so we gave his grandparents one of his bronzed boots. They use theirs in the same manner.

I have another treasure my grandfather gave me seventeen years ago: love letters my grandmother sent him back in 1930. They were buried for a long time in a candy box she gave him, but I dug them out. We've a replica of an old-fashioned writing desk with divers dividers across the back. My grandparents' love letters add an authentic antique touch to the replica.

Are you as nostalgic as one new bride who has saved every bouquet of flowers she's ever received from her boyfriend-turned-groom? Is there a sensible use for her sentimental sweet-smelling stems? She could press them between the pages of books; but, no, no. That would be too messy.

Here's a thought, though. She could put all her crumbling corsages and pressed petals into a clear, globular bowl (creating a precious pot of potpourri) and keep the fading flowers freshened up with drops of fragrant oils. Hopefully she'll be able to add to this sweet collection as her fine husband faithfully keeps the florist busy. He probably will when he sees how much his thoughtfulness has meant to her.

My sister-in-law Lynne Gallagher uses a family heirloom Singer sewing machine as a television table. The VCR equipment fits nicely on the foot pedal below. The ancient and the modern converge favorably.

Display and enjoy your keepsakes in decorative and functional ways. But don't be as bad as one lady. She excused her dusty house by this rationale: "The Bible says we were created from dust and will one day return to dust. You see, I don't want to disturb the dust around here," she said. "I kinda like having my ancestors around." She's a little too sentimental for me!

Don't be selfish; if you can't use the heirlooms you have, give them to a family member who can use and enjoy them.

COLLECTIONS

Luring advertisements and other marketing techniques bring a wide variety of collectibles to our attention. Our best advice is to "go easy" on collections. Put a quick quietus on this "snowball" before it rolls and rolls along, picking up quintillions of extras that will clutter your home.

Most customers order too many collectibles. Some of the categories aren't that meaningful either. In our children's weekly newspaper, I read about a man who collects beverage cans. The space "swallowed up" to store them was unbelievable. While I can't say his empty, hollow collection was meaningless for him, I certainly saw no inherent value in it for me.

Ladies collect dolls, plates, salt and pepper shakers, bells and a host of other things. Be selective with your collections.

Mother has a meaningful collection of baskets in her kitchen. (You've already decided I was a "basket case." And now you'll find out that my mother is a "basket case," too.)

In her big, country kitchen, hanging from the exposed beams is a bay of baskets that Daddy brought home from his travels. The churches who host his evangelistic meetings often put a fruit basket in his room; he brings the baskets home to Mother.

I've tried to curb you from wasteful collecting, but I'd like to challenge you to begin or continue collecting two worthy assortments. Each of us instinctively collects something. (I chuckle to think of the silly things I've gathered through the years.) Whatever we collect becomes a positive source of pleasure in our lives; if improperly prioritized, trite trinkets can become a negative point of pride.

First, collect wisdom. Doing so will make the highest use of your natural gathering instinct. Use a large, 8 1/2-by-11-inch notebook to gather wisdom. File your sacred collection under headings like: salvation, service, soul winning, prayer, giving or suffering. Categorize your thoughts, ideas, illustrations, quotes and verses. Make it your goal to collect as much wisdom as you can.

Second, build a personal library. Include an array of Bible study helps: a good commentary, a concordance, a Greek word study like Vine's or Thayer's, a Bible handbook like Halley's and a Bible dictionary like Unger's.

Start a collection of books on marriage, child training, housekeeping and time management. I am an interpreter for the deaf, so my library includes several sign language books. Being a pastor's wife, I collect books on the ministry.

Our children have their own personal libraries, too. They especially enjoy biographies; so do I. My father has challenged them to read biographies of great men. After reading and reporting on each book their Papa selects, the boys receive $20.00 from him. This is money well invested.

Our older son Alan has already surrendered his life to preach the Gospel of Jesus Christ. He made that profession at a National Sword of the Lord Conference. But I believe the inspiration of lives like Moody, Spurgeon and Sunday touched his heart even beforehand.

To add to his reading pleasure, we mounted an individual wall lamp beside each boy's bed. They're each allowed thirty minutes to read after they get in bed. They cover up in their cozy little covey and seem to look forward to this privilege.

Develop a dynamite library. But remember to eliminate and concentrate. Don't crowd your bookshelves with bindings just for their attractiveness. Spend your money on books that will serve as reference manuals for years to come.

ORDER IN THE COURT

There are reams of written material out there today; some are wastes of time and money and can be summarized in one sentence. I've been told that since 1960, the amount of printed or published material has doubled every ten years. So be selective and sensitive when building your library.

CAR

The care of our cars is actually the responsibility of the men of our house, though there are a few "telltale signs" that I've been around. Over the visor is an organizer with various compartments. Here's where I temporarily keep ATM receipts, dry cleaning receipts, shoe repair stubs, ticket stubs for parking and restaurant coupons.

Tracts are in one pouch and a daily devotional is in another. The many drive-through services are open opportunities to pass along tracts. The devotional is there, so if we find ourselves waiting again, we can read from it.

My husband's secretary secured "Clergy Cards" from all the local hospitals for both of us. What a blessing that is! Our passes are kept in this over-the-visor organizer also. These allow for complimentary parking, but the best benefit is the privilege to park in designated spots. We are required to lay the pass up in the window in order to park in the clergy section. Hospital parking lots are often crowded, and this pass has been a real help.

For your safety, you need to keep the following "helps" in the car: sunglasses (a must for me), maps, jumper cables, a first-aid kit, a blanket, a flashlight, a magnetic key case for concealing an extra key, and several quarters for emergency phone calls. An extra safety precaution is to drop a card (with your name, address and phone number on it) down into the car door through the window opening. If the car is ever stolen, you'll have a way to prove ownership.

For tidiness you'll need a small trash can, Kleenex and wetwipes. Carry a few small toys or games for when "the natives are restless."

COSMETICS AND PERSONAL HYGIENE

God asks for self-denial, not self-rejection. Grant time for your personal appearance. Your self-image is integral to every other relationship you'll experience.

Make that famous up-front investment of time by having your colors analyzed via a professional. She will look at your complexion and tell you what colors you wear most beautifully. This will limit your wardrobe to one basic color—black, brown or navy—and will put a natural limit on your spending.

Go for a complete look from head to toe, considering hairstyling, outfit, jewelry, purse and shoes. Winnow down your wardrobe to a few nice and complete outfits.

In sociology class, a startling truth was brought out; it stuck with me. When studying the social institutions, their strata and interactions, we learned about the three obvious classes: the upper, middle and lower.

Which two classes do you think are most alike? Which two classes are harder to distinguish between? Well, the middle class easily gives themselves away by their persnickety profusion—excess amounts of clothes and other materialistic pageantry.

The upper and lower classes have more close resemblances from a distance. They both have fewer clothes. Of course, the upper class wears very expensive and exorbitant attire, while the lower class dresses in modest and meager raiment. But they are alike in that they both flaunt fewer fashions.

Select a fragrant "trademark." Certain perfumes bring specific persons to mind, don't they? Anytime I "get a whiff" of White Linen, Mother's face comes to mind. If you use a light fragrance like mine, *L'air du Temp* by Nina Ricci, layering the aroma through the use of perfumed soap, lotion, powder, body splash and cologne lasts longer.

ORDER IN THE COURT

Carry a comfortable and capacious purse. I prefer a short-handled shoulder bag these days, because I need the extra hand for children. The purse fits right under my arm; it seems safe there.

To help keep your purse in order, use small, clear cosmetic bags. One can be for makeup and another can be a minioffice with pens and pencils, small scissors, paper clips, etc. Another bag can hold mints, medicines, etc. And another can be for loose change.

When you need to change purses, the process is easy. Transfer your pocket-sized Bible and those few bags into another purse.

To save drawer space in the bathroom, I started using a "Caboodle" to put away makeup and cosmetics. There is another benefit I hadn't anticipated. When it's time for a trip, some of the packing is already done. Cosmetics and travel-sized toiletries are already in the Caboodle.

CHILDREN

Children can be an efficient work force and can do a lot to help around the house. Together we (the children, Rick and I) laid out a list of reasonable responsibilities and daily chores. Naturally the list changes from time to time as the boys get older and stronger. It is printed out for them with boxes for checking off the finished jobs. This paper does my nagging for me; you realize what I mean. I don't have to keep telling them over and over; they are reminded of what they have to do each time they look at the list.

If this list is completely checked off Monday through Friday, they receive a monetary reward. Praise what is done well instead of criticizing what is not done well. Refrain from criticism; simply reteach what needs improvement.

Children can help even more with the right tools and amenities. Install shelves on their levels so they can put up their belongings with ease. Toy boxes are not the best way to store toys; shelves are a lot better. They can see everything and select one item without dumping out the entire contents of the toy chest.

Children can be wonderful hosts and hostesses. When their friends come over, I try to do a good job as hostess, offering a snack and drink. And they very favorably return this favor.

Just a few weeks ago our friends Kathy Taylor and her father, Mr. Goddard, were visiting in our home. I remember well how we had special prayer for Daddy that morning; he was at the doctor's office even as we prayed.

Alan was such a happy host, serving them iced tea. I was so pleased; I hadn't prompted him to do that. Children enjoy showing hospitality. What a gentleman-like gesture from my little guy! There was nothing sissy about it; boys can be little hosts, too.

COMPUTER

Most any job you do on paper can be done more efficiently on a personal computer. Recently I have discovered this "new world" for myself. One of my self-improvement goals is to take some computer classes and learn to operate new programs.

The programs I use now can help with many responsibilities we've already mentioned: addresses, finances, birthday greetings and letter writing. I've become quite dependent on this word processing program. I don't think I could write the "Children's Challenge," a regular column in THE SWORD OF THE LORD, without it now. Computers help us to work smarter, instead of harder.

CELEBRATIONS

Christmas: Establish family traditions, but don't try to implement each tradition every year. Besides a yummy traditional Southern-style dinner with all the trimmings and the exchanging of gifts, here are some of the ways we've celebrated Christmas through the years. Remember, we don't execute each of these ideas every year.

But I'll start with a few traditions that we do include annually. We make a birthday cake for Jesus every year on His birthday. One year the cake was shaped like a Lamb. The wording on it read: "Born to die."

No matter which side of the family we spend the holiday with, everyone "pitches in" to help with the Christmas cook-a-thon. The family always requests that I make an Italian Cream Cheese Cake. Christmas just wouldn't be Christmas without some things, now, would it?

I borrowed a fun tradition from my friend Brenda Turner. One red toothpick is hidden in the cake. The person who finds it in his piece of cake receives a gift from me. (The gift has to be suitable for any gender or age.) Now that is one way to get your cake eaten really fast!

One year the family of each Hutson sibling presented a short Christmas program for the entire Hutson clan—that's quite an audience before whom to perform. Some years we go caroling with the neighbors or church groups. We often adopt an inner-city family for the holidays, delivering food and gifts downtown. We've adopted missionary families, too.

Holiday greetings are sent out every other year, as explained. Selected years we attend cultural events like the Atlanta Symphony Orchestra's performance of Handel's *Messiah*. We've toured "The Festival of Trees" several years, where decorated trees from many different countries are on display. We've viewed an Atlanta tradition, the lighting of the big tree downtown.

One year we hang stockings on the mantel. Some years we begin gift-giving the twelve days before Christmas. For those twelve days, each child receives a small gift—very exciting and suspenseful.

When home with Mother and Daddy, we take a privately chartered trip to the beautiful OpryLand Hotel and catch one of the performances of their harpist. When Rick's parents lived in Orlando, we took in all the sights and sounds of Christmas at the "not-to-be-outdone" Disney World.

Just recalling these events and all the memories and blessings that came along with them floods my heart with thanks and my eyes with tears of joy. God has been so good to us!

Is it possible to be grieved over the giving of gifts? Yes, and this is the source of much holiday hassle and headache. Impose a deadline on yourself. Say, "I will have all gifts purchased by November 1 or whenever, Lord willing." Use your gift list to shop all year long for those items; buy them at sale prices. Set a price limit on each gift; this step alone will narrow down your choices and make purchases easier. The drawing of names will help manage the madness. Wrap your gifts early, as you buy them, with paper you bought last year at the "after Christmas" sale.

We love welcoming guests whom the holidays usher in through the front door. Dinner is not usually served, but cakes, candies and coffees are always offered.

Phew! What a production! Even without trying to do everything each year, I found myself being bogged down by *all* of the activities rather than enjoying *any* of them. I was trying to build so many memories for our children that I was missing out on that spontaneous spirit of Christmas. Surely you can empathize.

I would be frustrated and sad when the sun set on this very special holiday. I'd spent weeks, maybe months, planning and preparing. In one big but brief blast, it was all over. And I hadn't even taken time to play one game with the children. Although everything may have been in order, with food and festivities in abundance, I'd neglected the more important activities.

I felt a bit of hope when I realized no one was forcing us to end the celebration so abruptly. The week between Christmas and New Year's has become a very special time for our immediate family. All the parties and special church services are over, and the open houses are closed now. Cantata practices are finished, gifts have already been opened, but carols are still ringing. Guests—family and friends—are on their way back home, but some very important celebrities yet remain.

Breaking a Hutson family tradition, we leave our decorations up throughout this transitional week, as we turn another page on the calendar and welcome in a new year.

We snuggle together and enjoy all those treats we may have missed during the hustle and bustle of the weeks prior to Christmas—hot chocolate and soft cookies or shortbread, re-reading the Christmas story, playing with the new toys, and watching holiday videos.

This somewhat "lost" week is a new-found delight for us. A pastor is usually not in that much demand this particular week; it is a low-keyed few days for us. Rick had worked many extra hours those festive weeks before Christmas. We are "all together now," breathing that sigh of relief.

Birthdays: All our children were born in December, but in different decades. One was born in the 70's, one in the 80's, and one in the 90's. We really spread them out, didn't we? Our CPA thinks we are very smart tax planners!

But all those December birthdays add extra extravaganzas to this already busy month. We asked the Lord to open our eyes to see different ways in which we might celebrate these birthdays. He helped us, as He promised.

One year we celebrated their half-birthdays in the nice hot month of June when their friends were out of school. Another year we gave them parties on their spiritual birthdays. Alan and Curt gave their testimonies, and these were good ways to witness to the little boys in our neighborhood. Can you picture the little fellows trying to explain all this to their parents? Another witness for Jesus.

Use banners to make your loved ones feel special on their birthdays. One mother made a unique banner for each child, depicting his special interests and displaying his favorite colors. Attaching the banner to a flagpole, this mother was able to stand it in the ground just any day that particular child needed an "uplift," as well as on his birthday.

Be prepared for birthdays by keeping a pack of birthday candles in the pantry. Any cake can be turned into a birthday cake with candles.

Save the front pages of the newspapers on your children's birthdays. Office supply stores carry a box made to hold flattened newspapers; so I got one for each child. When the children are much older, they will appreciate this interesting walk back through time.

CHRISTLIKE

We've sailed through some rough "C's." Clutter, cleaning, cooking, clothing, closets, cosmetics, checkbook, calendar, centers, collections, cherished items, communications, computer, car, children and celebrations.

But this last "C" is a calm sea. I speak of Christ, the Master of the sea, whose "yoke is easy" and whose "burden is light" (Matthew 11:30). Enter into His sweet rest.

Hebrews chapter 4 speaks nine times about the Christian's rest. "There remaineth therefore a rest to the people of God. For he that is entered into his rest, he also hath ceased from his own works, as God did from his. Let us labour therefore to enter into that rest. . ." (Hebrews 4:9-11).

May I ask you a probing question? Is your home Christlike? When a visitor comes on your premises, will he see Christ in you and in your surroundings? Can one sense that Christ is always your Honored Guest? Does the Holy Spirit have complete reign in your castle?

What can you do to make the atmosphere of your abode Christlike? Begin with "Order in the Heart." Is your heart cleansed by the blood of Jesus? Is your heart controlled by the Holy Spirit? Is your heart content, cheerful and contrite?

There will be outward evidences of those inward experiences. Your actions will reveal the changes of the heart.

ORDER IN THE COURT

Your home can also reflect the joy of the Lord. Hang Scriptures in cross-stitch or calligraphy throughout the house.

In our foyer hang cross-stitched name graphs of each family member. Starting at the top is "JESUS: Saviour." "And thou shalt call his name JESUS: for he shall save his people from their sins" (Matthew 1:21). Next is "Camperson." ". . .but as for me and my house, we will serve the Lord" (Joshua 24:15). Following is Rick, Sherry, Alan and Curt. And finally "Jana Kay: God's Gracious Gift." "And therefore will the Lord wait, that he may be gracious unto you, and therefore will he be exalted. . .blessed are all they that wait for him" (Isaiah 30:18). We waited fourteen years for our little daughter. What a fitting verse has been attached to her beautiful name!

We have chosen Isaiah 30:18 as our family verse, too. God has placed us in His "waiting room" for some time now. We gladly wait that He may be exalted.

Other verses are obscurely placed throughout the house. They're for our own warnings and encouragements. An appropriate verse is laminated on the alarm clock, "As for me, I. . .shall be satisfied, when I awake, with thy likeness" (Psalm 17:15). On one of the bathroom mirrors is this verse, "But be ye doers of the word, and not hearers only, deceiving your own selves. For if any be a hearer of the word, and not a doer, he is like unto a man beholding his natural face in a glass: For he beholdeth himself, and goeth his way, and straightway forgetteth what manner of man he was" (James 1:22-24).

Choose verses you love and wish to live by. Post them on the doors and windows of your house (Deuteronomy 11:18-22).

The year-round display of our nativity scene adds to a Christlike appearance. We enjoy our manger scene all year. It is a very lovely one, and the children have always loved playing with it. It's sure to be one of their imbedded childhood memories. Over the nativity hangs a beautiful needlework by

74

a dear lady of our church: "His name shall be called Wonderful, Counsellor, The mighty God, The everlasting Father, The Prince of Peace" (Isaiah 9:6).

The Bible should be clearly seen, occupying an honored place. When books are stacked on a table or bookcase, I want the Bible to be the Book on top. I'm especially insulted if a TV magazine is lying on top of the blessed Bible.

Make your castle Christlike by lifting high the "Royal Standard." The "Royal Standard" flies over the palace when the King is in residence. Is the King at home in your house? Can your guests detect His presence?

NATURAL ENEMIES OF ORDER

Our final strategic plan is the exposure of order's natural enemies. These are foes that have held me hostage from time to time.

1. The flesh. Trying to do your work in the energy of the flesh results in what is commonly called "burnout." In the June 1990 issue of *Human Resources* magazine, a business publication, there was an article in the wellness section by Dr. Hugh Stallwork on the subject of burnout. He gave this clinical definition that convicted my heart as a born-again Christian. You will understand why I felt convicted. Dr. Stallwork said, "Burnout is the perception that a person is giving more than he/she is receiving whether it is money, praise or satisfaction."

But the Bible says, 'Serve and do good, hoping for nothing again' (Luke 6:31-35). Convicted once more. So if a person gives and works expecting nothing in return, the pain of burnout will be diminished. Are you experiencing the "burnout syndrome"?

Syndrome simply means a collection of symptoms. Burnout is only a symptom, not the root problem. Burnout occurs when you are trying to perform in your weak flesh what can only be done through the inexhaustible power of the Holy Spirit. If we serve God and others through this inextinguishable Fire Power, we cannot burn out. Truly the flesh is weak, but the spirit is renewed every day (II Corinthians 4:16).

2. Obsessive service. Learn when and how to say "No" in the right manner, without sounding angry, frustrated or uncaring. *No* is not a four-letter word. If you are being pressured into a commitment, the best answer is "No." And no matter how clear the calendar may look at the moment, ask for a day or two to pray for guidance. Withstand the urgency of that pleading voice, and you'll have the time to discern whether the task is God's will for you. Remember, *no* is not a bad word; it may even be the most important word in the Christian vocabulary. It is simply amazing how many ways I can distract my own self when I'm trying to avoid what I should be doing but don't want to do. Learn to say "No" to yourself, also. Oswald Chambers said, "Action is no substitute for production."

3. Love of pleasure. Hedonism is the doctrine that pleasure is the chief goal in life. We are an Epicurean society, preoccupied with pleasing ourselves. We escape into pleasure different ways. Some sneak away through sleep, TV, reading, daydreaming, shopping or just leaving the house and all their responsibilities behind. "He that loveth pleasure shall be a poor man. . ." (Proverbs 21:17). Ken Collier of the Wilds Christian Retreat posed our proposition in this poetic phrase: "Only two choices on the shelf: pleasing God or pleasing self."

4. Workaholism. Women who work outside the home aren't the only women who can become obsessed with their work. Women who are full-time, stay-at-home moms rarely have time for their creative projects. Mothering and homemaking are forty-eight-hour-per-day jobs. If one is a workaholic, she can *always find* something to do.

A most natural enemy of order is that weakening exhaustion caused by the compulsive behavior of workaholics. Your body needs rest. When one is physically weak, she is more susceptible to emotional and spiritual attacks. Jesus wants to share our work load.

Jonathan experienced great victory over the Philistines in I Samuel 14 because the 'Lord worked for him' (I Samuel 14:6). God wants to give rest to the workaholic. "Come unto me, all ye that labour and are heavy laden, and I will give you rest" (Matthew 11:28). "It is time for thee, Lord, to work. . ." (Psalm 119:126). The Lord wants to work with you. "And they went forth, and preached every where, the Lord working *with* them. . ." (Mark 16:20).

5. **Indecisiveness.** The inability to make decisions can be defeating. Often folks grow up feeling their decisions were never right, so it has become less painful to postpone or totally neglect decisions than to risk making the wrong one again. Indecision is draining on a person. If you wait, the decision will be made for you. I've heard it said this way: "Deal with the situation, or be dealt with by it." Past failures often result in a bad self-image. Set new goals and go after them. ". . .forgetting those things which are behind, and reaching forth unto those things which are before, I press toward the mark. . ." (Philippians 3:13,14).

6. **Procrastination.** This threat to an orderly life is both stressful and distressful. There is a difference between *stress* and *distress*. The Bible uses the word *distress*, not *stress*. Stress is pressure from without; distress is pressure from within, which is the more destructive strain. Don't allow yourself to become the victim of this adversary. Whatever you want to do tomorrow, do today. Whatever you want to do today, do now. An English proverb says, "What can be done anytime is never done at all."

7. **Perfectionism.** A mother's perfectionism can make for an unhappy home. I was convicted by a very sad article entitled "My Mommy's a Perfectionist."

Perfectionism is a case where "lowering your standards" can be good and right. I heard a cute story with which you can identify, I'm sure. Have you ever heard your hungry husband hunting around in the refrigerator for something to hush his hankering for food? One man was scrapping for just any ol' scrap he could find. He left the kitchen a defeated man. A little later he returned to the refrigerator to ransack it again. "You've already gone through the Frigidaire once, Dear. You know there's nothing good to eat," chided his wife. With a mouthful of something, he muttered, "I've lowered my standards." We may be wise to try that sometimes, too.

A perfectionist truly "can't see the forest for the trees." That one spends too much time on each project. The perfectionist becomes a disorderly person because she doesn't have enough time to do every job extremely well. She radically lives by the old adage, "A job worth doing is worth doing well." If she can't do it unequivocally well, she won't do it at all.

Edwin Bliss said, "There is a difference between striving for excellence and striving for perfection. The first is attainable, gratifying and healthy; the second is unattainable, frustrating and neurotic. It is a terrible waste of time." (Again I confess that I'm a "recovering perfectionist," but I am making progress in my rehabilitation process.)

8. Worry. How much time we waste by worrying! Daddy always says, "Worry is like a rocking chair. It gives you something to do but doesn't get you anywhere."

My husband tells me there are *only two things* I can't worry about. He says, "Don't worry about things you can change; and don't worry about things you can't change." He wisely covered it all. If you *can* change the situation, just do it and stop worrying. If you *can't* change the situation, accept it and stop worrying. Satan can succeed to stump you if you worry. He knows you can ruin a perfectly good present by worrying about a poor past. "Worry is using today's strength on tomorrow's problems" (Dr. Curtis Hutson).

9. Traditions. Be willing to learn and try new ideas. Don't be stranded on the road to progress by carrying on meaningless traditions. I heard a story about a newlywed couple. Every time the bride cooked a roast, her first step in preparation was to cut off the shank end and then put the remainder of the roast in the pot. After watching this ritual many times, her groom asked why she did it. "That's the way my mother always did it" was her reply. "Why?" he asked. "I don't know," she said. "Well, why don't you ask her why?" he persisted. So the puzzled wife called her mother and asked why she always cut off the end of the roast. The mother answered, "Oh, that's because my pan is too small." Imagine how much good meat, time and money was wasted because of blindly following a hollow tradition.

10. **Sentimentalism.** "Guilty, guilty," I confess again. And I can testify that, when given no boundaries and so taken to the extreme, sentimentality is an enemy of order, and it has other negative effects. Keeping everything because of our emotional attachment will result in a very cluttered life. Keepsakes are important, but you can't keep everything. Someone said, "Don't love anything that can't love you back."

These are natural enemies of order. Resist their tepid temptations. Flee from them. Don't get caught in their trusty trappings.

❂ ❂ ❂ ❂ ❂

What about interruptions and hindrances? Oh, did I forget to mention them on that list of enemies? No, that didn't slip my mind. The omission was deliberate. For a long time I viewed interruptions and hindrances as wicked enemies to order, but I was wrong.

On the contrary, all interruptions and hindrances are "according to the good hand of my God" (Nehemiah 2:8). God makes better plans than the best time manager or schedule strategist. It's been said, "The 'stops' as well as the 'steps' of a good man are ordered by the Lord."

My husband recently preached a message entitled "Hindrances Are Helps," while teaching a series through the book of Genesis. This lesson was learned from the life of one of my favorite Bible characters. Joseph's plans were postponed by interruptions and hindrances with which he had nothing to do. But as was pointed out, his interruptions were not happening "to him," but rather "for him."

The verse we've heard emphasized is "God meant it unto good, to bring it to pass. . ." (Genesis 50:20). The word *meant* there is also the word *woven*. God wove every hindrance in his life for Joseph's good and to bring his (and His) every goal and plan to pass. Alexander Maclaren said, "Not one thread of the tapestry of Joseph's life could have been withdrawn without spoiling the entire pattern."

With that in mind, welcome interruptions and hindrances. They are sent from God. I'm deeply moved and comforted by these words from Alan Redpath:

> There is nothing—no circumstance, no trouble, no testing—that can ever touch me until first of all it has gone past God and past Christ right through to me. If it has come that far, it has come with great purpose which I may not understand at the moment. But as I refuse to become panicky, as I lift up my eyes to Him and accept it as coming from the throne of God for some great purpose of blessing to my own heart, no sorrow will ever disarm me, no circumstance shall cause me to fret, for I shall rest in the joy of what my Lord is, that is, the rest of victory.

Hindrances are helps.

"The world does not require so much to be informed as to be reminded" (Hannah Moore). So let me remind you that one cannot live in a haphazard manner and pray that everything will come out right in the end. The ideas and suggestions shared here are offered to you for your selective use. You will probably never use all of them, and you'll certainly not use them all at once.

Each job you tackle as a woman will require its own "set of tools." But instead of cramming your hands full by grabbing for all these tools at once, which will essentially halt your work, just pick up that one "tool" that best fits your hand. Try it, and see how it works.

But tools are only tools. They must be plugged into the right power source. Draw on the power of Christ within you and make those "home improvements" a little at a time. God will encourage and reward your every effort in search of order and peace. He will welcome your company, for His abode is order and peace. And you will find greater enjoyment in living.

And be reminded that "duties never conflict" (Bob Jones, Sr.). There is no level of organization high enough and no management of time strict enough to grant any individual a proficient performance of tasks that God did not assign. Maybe you haven't checked with God's plans, and you've taken on responsibilities that don't belong to you. Pray and ask God to reveal ways of paring down your projects. If your juggling act is getting "out of hand," watch out. You're about to get hit in the head. Simplify your life as best you can.

I've prayed that this time together and our inner communication (although I'm sorry it could only be a "one-way conversation") has been an encouragement to you. If you still feel in any little way overwhelmed or frustrated, please let me perk you up with another shot of "vitamin E," that is, Encouragement.

It is not how far you've traveled that matters; it's the direction in which you are headed. The mere fact that you have sought help by picking up a book on this subject indicates that you are headed in the right direction. Where you are on the road to order does not matter; just move at God's pace.

Start somewhere. One can have the most expensive stationery from Eaton's or Crane's Collection—bonded, watermarked, 100% rag or deckle-edged—the finest Mont Blanc writing instrument and a supply of stamps and still not write a letter. One can have an exhaustive library and never read a book.

I was comforted and encouraged when I realized that

ORDER IN THE COURT

Proverbs 31 is not a listing of the Ideal Woman's daily activities. No—she didn't get up before the sun, purchase a nice piece of property, plant a vineyard, make bread, shop for wool and flax, then weave cloth, stitch the children's clothes, run errands for her husband, take food to the hungry, market her fine linen, look like a million dollars, speak sagely and stay up all night—each and every day of her life.

Proverbs 31:10-31 is a summary of her entire life! I don't feel guilty anymore, and neither should you. There were seasons to her life, just as there are seasons to our lives.

I remember those less crowded days when I was a career single; and I look back on them with a satisfied feeling of accomplishment, as I loved my work. Then came the new challenges of marriage and setting up housekeeping; and those memories are sweet, special and sacred to me. As God bestowed each of three children, the blessings and burdens increased proportionately; and we are building beautiful memories now. "My plate is getting fuller."

After what I know was a lifetime of "on-the-job training" as a PK (preacher's kid), God changed the seasons again. He made His will clear for my husband to start a church. And here again, this "birthing" required "labor pains" of its own variety and intensity. And this "new life," too, brought with it more blessings and burdens—*still* in equal proportions. God knows how to balance perfectly the burdens He puts on our backs and the blessings He places in our hands. The memories of this rewarding ministry are of the immortal type, as people are born again and lives are forever changed. There are other seasons to come when God, in His time, will paint a different canvas of beauty.

Shakespeare said, "Life is made of seven stages." He may have been right about that, as seven is God's number for perfection. God wants to see His perfect will completed in you. He will give you enough time to do everything He has planned for you to do. "Being confident of this very thing, that he which hath begun a good work in you will perform it until the day of Jesus Christ" (Philippians 1:6).

FOR FURTHER READING

Aslett, Don. *Clutter's Last Stand*. Writer's Digest Books.

Aslett, Don. *Do I Dust or Vacuum First?* Writer's Digest Books.

Aslett, Don. *Is There Life After Housework?* Video available. Writer's Digest Books.

Aslett, Don. *Stain Busters Bible: The Complete Guide to Spot Removal*. Plume Books.

Barnes, Emilie. *Survival for Busy Women*. Eugene, Oregon: Harvest House Pub.

Begoun, Paula. *Blue Eyeshadow Should Be Illegal*. Beginning Press.

Burkett, Larry. *Financial Planning Organizer*. Victor Publishers.

Burkett, Larry. *Financial Planning Workbook*. Victor Publishers.

Burkett, Larry. *Investing for the Future*. Victor Publishers.

Christenson, Evelyn. *Gaining Through Losing*. Victor Publishers.

Christenson, Evelyn. *Lord, Change Me*. Victor Publishers.

Collins, Gary. *Handling the Holidays*.

Culp, Stephanie. *Conquering the Paper Pileup*. Writer's Digest Books.

Culp, Stephanie. *How to Conquer Clutter*. Cincinnati, Ohio: Writer's Digest Books.

Culp, Stephanie. *How to Get Organized—When You Don't Have Time*. Writer's Digest Books.

Culp, Stephanie. *Organized Closets and Storage*. Writer's Digest Books.

Culp, Stephanie. *Streamlining Your Life*. Writer's Digest Books.

DiAntonia, Steve. *Making Time*. Ballantine Books.

Felton, Sandra. *The Messies Manual* (Parts 1 and 2). Fleming H. Revell Co.

Fulton, Alice, and Pauline Hatch. *It's Here Somewhere*. Writer's Digest Books.

Hummel, Charles E. *Tyranny of the Urgent*. InterVarsity

Press.

Hunter, Brenda. *Home by Choice*. Portland, Oregon: Multnomah Press.

Jackson, Carole. *Color Me Beautiful*. Random House Publisher.

Lawhead, Alice Slaiken. *The Christmas Book*. Crossway Books.

Mackenzie, R. Alec. *The Time Trap*. McGraw Hill.

McCollough, Bonnie. *Bonnie's Household Organizer*. St. Martin's Press.

McCollough, Bonnie, and Susan Monson. *401 Ways to Get Your Kids to Work at Home*. St. Martin's Press.

McCollough, Bonnie. *Totally Organized*. St. Martin's Press.

Miller, Ruth. *The Time Minder*.

Ortlund, Anne. *Disciplines of the Beautiful Woman*. Word Books.

Ortlund, Anne. *Disciplines of the Heart*. Word Books.

Ortlund, Ray and Anne. *Staying Power*. Oliver Nelson Pub.

Peel, Kathy, and Judie Byrd. *A Mother's Manual for Holiday Survival*. Focus on the Family Publishing.

Schofield, Deniece. *Confessions of a Happily Organized Family*. Writer's Digest Books.

Schofield, Deniece. *Confessions of an Organized Housewife*. Writer's Digest Books.

Sprinkle, Patricia. *Women Who Do Too Much*. Zondervan.

Stafford, Alexander. *The Gift of a Letter*.

Whelchel, Mary. *The Christian Working Woman*. Fleming H. Revell Co.

Young, Pam, and Peggy Jones. *Catch-up on the Kitchen*. Warner Books.

Young, Pam, and Peggy Jones. *Side-Tracked Home Executives*. Warner Books.

Young, Pam, and Peggy Jones. *The Side-Tracked Sister's Happiness File*. Warner Books.

While these books contain valuable information on their specific subject matter, neither this author nor publisher can endorse all contents.